NOT ALIENS

primary school children and the Citizenship/PSHE curriculum

Hilary Claire

NOT ALIENS
primary school children and the Citizenship/PSHE curriculum

Hilary Claire

Trentham Books
Stoke on Trent, UK and Sterling, USA

Trentham Books Limited
Westview House
734 London Road
Oakhill
Stoke on Trent
Staffordshire
England ST4 5NP

22883 Quicksilver Drive
Sterling
VA 20166-2012
USA

First published 2001

British Library Cataloguing-in-Publication Data
A catalogue record for this book is available from the British Library

1 85856 242 2

Designed and typeset by Trentham Print Design Ltd., Chester and printed in Great Britain by Cromwell Press Ltd., Wiltshire.

Contents

In memory of Gilli Slater and Joyce Kelly, women of compassion.

And dedicated to Eddie Funde and Willy 'Ntinyan' Matabane, courageous friends from the past who are working for a better future.

Acknowledgements and thanks

To all the children who talked to me, the teachers in both schools and especially the headteacher of 'Sylvia Pankhurst School', who must all remain anonymous

to Jack, for always being ready to listen, discuss and help me develop my ideas, and supporting me with resources and technology

to Gillian Klein, for believing in this book, for funny reassuring emails and for judicious editing

to Sue Adler of the Islington Library and Resources Service, and Mai Kim Stern and Sally Hill of Letterbox Library, for their time and help

to Phil Salmon and the members of Phil's Ph.D seminar group, who shared their interpretations of some the children's transcripts with me

to my brother Jon Blair, for his sensitivity and care in taking the cover photograph.

Introduction

This book is unashamed in its objectives. It aims to empower teachers and student teachers. It is for those of you who have felt deskilled and demoralised by the narrowly prescriptive bureaucracy of numeracy and literacy hours, Standard Assessment Tests and target setting, and have wondered whether there is any space left for creative teaching which helps children come to grips with ideas about their world. That we have Personal, Social, Health Education/Citizenship guidelines and not a statutory curriculum in the primary school is a godsend. We should grasp this opportunity to develop a transformative curriculum with our pupils.

Democracy is too important to be taught by prescription and we all know about death by worksheets. *Not Aliens* is written to help you interpret the official agenda of PSHE, 'Values Education' and Citizenship so that you can provide educational opportunities and mediate children's learning in the light of other children's ideas and concerns.

My view, sometimes called a 'maximalist approach', is that 'active citizenship' can be summarised as

EMPOWERMENT	Having the confidence and personal ability to take an active participant role – having a 'voice' and being heard
EMPATHY	Being able to understand one's own and other people's feelings, empathise when necessary and see other people's point of view
IDENTITY	Seeing where you fit in personally, having and gaining a sense of your identity as a member of a local, national and international community, and a strong sense that your own issues can be, and are, addressed

DIVERSITY	Knowing about the diversity of issues that affect citizens, from the very local to the global, even if these issues are not personal to you
ETHICS	Having an ethical framework for deciding between conflicting interests, in order to make sound, just judgements
ACTION	Having the opportunity to learn about citizenship and democracy through 'doing it' in real live projects
VISION	Having a sense of what a better community or world would look like and having the opportunity to debate this and to try and implement change in appropriate settings.

All these concepts are explored in this book.

The title *Not Aliens* has two connotations. Firstly, it is about everyone's right to citizenship, including people like 11 year old Ibrahim, who told me about the racism he encountered, saying 'we're not aliens, we're human beings'. Secondly, the children's voices in this book show that they share the adult world. They are not separate, innocent or different kinds of human being. Before we can take citizenship and PSHE seriously, we must find ways for the school curriculum to relate to their real knowledge and concerns with the world they share with adults.

The first five chapters take you into the minds and worlds of 34 children aged between 7 and 11, growing up and going to school in inner London. The final chapters draw innovatively on ideas from political theory, moral philosophy and economics to explore ways to develop the citizenship curriculum, taking on the issues and controversies the children introduced but also going beyond them. Each chapter concludes with ways forward for teachers.

Although the children were in Key Stage 2, Key Stage 1 and Key Stage 3 teachers will find plenty that is helpful and relevant, because actual experience is often more indicative of children's capabilities than chronological age. Most of the children were from ethnic minorities, most working class. They talked to me over several hours about their experiences, their concerns and what they wanted to change in their lives. The fundamental issues of the PSHE/citizenship guidance were at the heart of their talk – identity, self-esteem, concern about racism, resolving conflict in their immediate lives. If democracy is to mean anything, people's own agenda must be recognised, not straitjacketed or patronised. This book challenges preconceptions about what children of 'this age' know and think about. Their voices offer insights into the maturity and depth of understanding of children who are often patronised or silenced. Maud Blair (1998) talks about 'a listening school' – one which has a chance of being democratic – where children learn to find their own voice. I hope listening to these voices will help you when you listen to children in your own class.

Chapter 1 introduces the children and the ways I worked with them, making links between what you can do as a teacher and what I did as a researcher. I discuss the difference in knowledge and experience of working-class and ethnic minority children living on large estates, and the few middle-class children I interviewed, largely protected from the harsh lived realities of their classmates. I explain how I analysed the transcripts; my approach to children's talk is not 'academic ivory tower' but designed to help teachers understand their pupils.

Like the Guidance itself, Chapter 2 starts with children's self-esteem. Building on accepted thinking about the importance of the family, I show how children are regularly undermined by verbal abuse of their families, and particularly stereotypes of economic and social failure in society. I offer examples of children's self-insight and insight into other children, since this may be the key to dispelling ignorance and vindictiveness.

Chapter 3 builds on these ideas, moving on to identity – personal and national. The racism and religious intolerance experienced by many children raises serious questions about national identity, democracy and citizenship education. However, many children spoke powerfully against racism, drawing on wider knowledge than the school seemed to provide, and a sense of human rights and common humanity. It is essential to work with these concepts in addition to multiculturalism.

Chapter 4 explores education for personal health and safety. Even the youngest (working class) children had some knowledge of drug abuse in their neighbourhoods. Fear of child abuse was quite common among boys as well as girls, and two girls discussed the dangers of sexual exploitation and prostitution. As in the previous two chapters, I emphasise the importance of knowing what one's pupils already know and think about, to address their anxieties and prepare them appropriately for a safe and healthy future.

Chapter 5 briefly analyses children's understanding of economics and global citizenship. Their apparent lack of concern and knowledge replicates the way the school curriculum ignores economic understanding and global concerns. Chapter 7 returns to these themes with suggestions for development.

Chapter 6 is about values in education and particularly values in a democracy. I review the contributions of circle time, Philosophy for Children and emotional literacy and offer a framework for children to work with ideas about justice, rights, responsibilities, care and compassion, based in current philosophical and moral thinking. As part of the project to empower children and teachers, this chapter includes a section on decision-making, first at a personal level and then going wider in the school, to prepare the ground for responsible citizenship in the wider community.

Chapter 7 is called 'Tools for thinking' and seeks to break new ground in books for primary teachers. Children's misconceptions and misunderstandings and the limitations of the official curriculum indicate that there is a gap in citizenship education. Economics underpins all political decision-making and international relationships, and I offer teachers some starting points for children to understand the economic concepts which govern decisions about funding in a welfare economy. The chapter includes an overview of global issues which children might consider. It extends the practical examples for decision-making introduced in Chapter 6 and discusses resources and approaches offered by NGOs.

The final section lists a variety of resources, including web-sites, adult reading, activity packs, poetry and fiction to support the themes explored in this book.

1

The children, the issues, the method of working

In the late 1990s I worked with Key Stage 2 children in two inner London primary schools, one to the east – 'Mary Seacole' – and the other to the west – 'Sylvia Pankhurst'. I knew both schools through my work as a lecturer in primary education in London. Both are group 4 schools, housed in Victorian buildings dating from the 1890s, and both had a variety of recent conversions and improvements to their grounds and interiors. Both schools had teachers from ethnic minority groups as well as from the white majority, though only Sylvia Pankhurst School had any male teachers in the juniors. Each is the main neighbourhood school for a large new council estate close by, which I have called the Pankhurst and the Seacole Estates respectively. Not all children came from the estates. Some also lived in houses – sometimes subdivided into flats – and some lived in other smaller estates. Some children talked about the difference between living on one of the large estates or in a street of conventional older houses, or in different smaller estates, like the Peabody.

About 80% of the children in Sylvia Pankhurst School came from ethnic minority groups, and for many English was an additional language. There were many refugees and at that time 60% of the children were on the Free School Meals register. Sylvia Pankhurst had more Asian, African and Southern European children than Mary Seacole, though both had significant numbers of African-Caribbean, Turkish and Greek children. At Mary Seacole, 27% were from ethnic minority groups (about half of these neither African nor African-Caribbean), and 38% of the roll was on Free School Meals.

I chose Sylvia Pankhurst because I knew about its community and the school's commitment to equality issues and concern to provide a supportive ethos for children and parents. I had no prior knowledge about the Pankhurst Estate other than that many children lived there, or the issues that would be introduced by the children about the estate.

The real difference between the two schools relates to social class. The range of controversial social issues and knowledge introduced by the working-class children in Sylvia Pankhurst was very obvious at the point when I was considering a second school. Since Mary Seacole also had a large estate nearby and a significant number of ethnic minority and working-class children, I could test whether such issues would come up again. I had also become interested in how far class was determining the agenda raised by children. Unlike Sylvia Pankhurst School, Mary Seacole has a substantial minority of white middle-class children, and I ensured that they were represented in the sample. Comparing the interviews with the middle-class children and those from the majority working-class and ethnic minority children provides an illuminating perspective on the children's different experiences, concerns and knowledge. It was through analysing the content – and above all the gaps – in the white middle-class children's interviews that I started to speculate on the extent to which the prescribed PSHE/citizenship curriculum is underpinned by an implicit assumption that middle-class and/or white children are the norm in our schools.

Choosing the children

I wanted a balance of girls and boys, a representation of the actual ethnic composition of the schools, and in Mary Seacole, a representative proportion of middle-class children. I asked each class teacher to nominate a child (a boy, girl, ethnic minority child, middle-class child) to keep the composition of my sample roughly as I hoped, and left it to them. Each child they nominated was then asked to choose a close friend to be interviewed with them. When I started the research in Sylvia Pankhurst School, I had asked teachers to nominate pairs of children who were friends. The result produced an interesting perspective both on teachers' implicit value systems and also on their true knowledge of their class. Two teachers sent a boy-girl pair who, both assured me, were friends, and I proceeded with the interviews. It emerged that the teachers considered mixed-sex pairs as an important equal opportunities principle and assumed that was what I wanted. At the end of their interviews I asked the children whether they were really close friends and all four said they were not, though they got on reasonably well. I then asked each to nominate a close friend so we could do the interviews again. As a result, I had two sets of transcripts, based on the same questions but with each child in two settings. Though there were some overlaps in material, it was plain that in the teacher-chosen pairs the children were significantly more restrained, watchful even, about how they expressed themselves. I have not used any of the teacher-chosen pair interviews in this book. Only one self-chosen pair, Assia and Sean, is mixed sex. However, as the grid on page 16 shows, the majority of friendship pairs were ethnically mixed.

Before we began recording, I explained fully what I was doing, invited the children to question me about the research and made sure they were happy to be interviewed. One pair of boys in Sylvia Pankhurst did not want to stay and so they went back to class. The heads did not feel that parental permission was necessary. All the other children were keen to be part of this research (perhaps glad to be out of class!). They asked when I was coming back and several said how special they felt.

The Interviews

First a word about the feminist research approach which determines my work: feminist research strives for objectivity but does not pretend, or even encourage the attempt, to be neutral about issues. Rather, it asks researchers to be reflexive about who we are, what our values are, and how our presence affects the material we are collecting. This reflexivity is also important to teachers who know that relationships with their pupils are at the heart of a learning community.

The purpose of the research was to find out what was important to the children themselves, not to set an agenda for them. Nonetheless, the questions for the interviews (see Appendix) reflect my interest in children's own concerns and feelings. I wanted to know what children cared about, what they hoped to change both in and out of school. The overall purpose for my work is openly radical and emancipatory. With the PSHE/Citizenship already heralded, I could see an opportunity for rethinking aspects of the primary curriculum, moving beyond its increasingly technicist, instrumental approaches, and acknowledging that education should be about values, empowerment and feelings, as well as numeracy, literacy and preparation for work. A radical agenda should be informed by a sense of what children themselves think, understand and know, and not just top-down induction from a set of prescriptive curriculum 'oughts'. I wanted to work in inner-city schools because the curriculum they experience in areas of belief, value and social experience must be designed for them, relevant to *their* lives, and not assume they inhabit safe, suburban worlds. Though I was aware that racism and crime were all around them, I needed to find out whether this was the children's perception rather than mine. After all, the overt school curriculum currently behaves as if children were protected from the social pathology of the environments they live in, and so justifies excluding from its domain the controversial, difficult issues of society.

The emphasis in the questions on 'concern', 'care' and 'change' is deliberate but a warning goes with them. Though I did ask children what made them happy and what they enjoyed, the interviews mainly probed what they cared about, were concerned about, and would like to change in their lives. I also asked about conflict – fights in their personal experience and conflict in the wider world. This was because I wanted to get a feel for their understanding of the causes and nature of conflict, in the local, national and international field, which I see as contributing to the development of a curriculum for local, national and international citizenship. The result could be a view that the children live in a nightmarish world of hostility and violence. However, I am assuming that people reading this book are already familiar with some of the other issues that engage children's interests and discourse – the pop groups, the sport, the gossip, the local fashions. This book aims to provide insights into more intimate and arguably more significant issues in their lives.

Ways of working

The importance of friendship pairs and of the adult presence

A context and process which empowers children and leads to honesty and sincerity has enormous relevance for teachers in their own work. None of us behaves in quite the same way in a large group as we do on our own or with a trusted friend. When I was doing the pilot work for this study in a school in South London, I tried and abandoned three different approaches, and settled on the fourth. I started off by interviewing mixed-sex groups of six children, nominated by their teachers. I found, as others have done, that the boys dominated the discussion. I then tried single-sex groups of six children, containing both white and ethnic minority children, and finally, a single-sex group of six black children (African-Caribbean and African). Issues about sexism in school had arisen in the mixed-sex group, but the discussion flickered out. However, the single-sex girls' group raised and discussed their experience of sexism from teachers and boys with considerable detail and feeling. Racism was not introduced in the group when white children were present, but the group of black children talked at length about their experiences of racism; the same black children were present in both groups.

In the pilot interviews, an issue of confidentiality arose which alerted me to the fact that the size of the group and the presence of trustworthy others might affect what children would talk about. I had completed the interview and sent the children back to class, but two girls who were friends lingered. One started to tell me about events in her reconstituted family, which sounded to me like child abuse. I followed this up on a personal level. But I also decided that pairs of children were more likely than bigger groups to provide a safe environment that would permit disclosures of confidential material. Pragmatically, it is also easier to transcribe tapes with two children than with six.

There is another methodological issue which teachers might find interesting, working as they have to in much larger groups and under time constraints. At the start of the research I asked children if they would like to discuss some of the questions without me present but with the tape-recorder running. Two pairs chose this option. However, the material on these tapes was severely truncated. The children interpreted the written questions pretty much like a worksheet. They gave simple one-word or one-sentence answers and seemed to treat this as a task to be got through. They gave no more of themselves and seemed no more relaxed and open without me, though this might have changed under different circumstances when their anonymity was assured. These parts of the tape differed markedly from the talk generated in my presence. In a subsequent interview I asked both pairs if I might go back over some of the things they'd said on the tape they'd made without me, and because I was able to probe further and even take on a 'devil's advocate' role or role-play with them, these interviews were far more interesting and valuable. The conclusion seems to be that the children actually enjoyed developing their thoughts with an interested adult and benefited from the feedback. Some children said that it was unusual and a privilege to have an adult devote concentrated time to their ideas and opinions. Many people have noted that children are seldom asked in school what they think about things, let alone invited to talk about their concerns and set their own agenda. The challenge for teachers is how to replicate conditions in which children feel comfortable enough to be open, are not restricted by being in a group that is too large for sincerity or by the dynamics of interpersonal relationships. If I am right about the importance of adult interaction with small groups of children, teachers have to consider how to organise their own availability, instead of relying on plenaries which do not facilitate the airing of views or thoughtful discussion.

My part in creating the transcripts

Though I was not in the role of a teacher, and explained about the research and what I was doing, all the children knew that I was a teacher in another life. Though I had a 'script' of open-ended questions, I gave them the opportunity to start where they wanted, to ask anything about me and what I was doing, and to contribute questions that they would like to answer. I tried to be sensitive and responsive to what the children were telling me. I moved on if they seemed uncomfortable with a question, or had nothing more to say. On the other hand, I followed up issues that I felt needed clarification, asking the children to say more, or to explain what they meant. I often repeated back to them what they had said, asking if I'd got it right and giving them an opportunity to correct me, expand or change their argument if they wanted to. This is part of qualitative interviewing technique and will be familiar to teachers using their power to ask for clarification and elucidation of ideas. I used role-play, acted as devil's advocate and invited children to argue with me or with each other. Some children, particularly the younger ones, really enjoyed this, and asked to 'do this game' of arguing with me. Where I was perhaps unlike a teacher was in sitting back and listening to children talking with each other, without interrupting. This generated some of the most illuminating interchanges, where I could genuinely see children developing their thinking jointly and moving each other on.

Teachers are unlikely to be collecting transcripts or having time to analyse them. However, your long-term, concentrated contact with children gives you an advantage I did not have, in appreciating your pupils' knowledge, feelings and understandings. My hope, in making transparent both the ways the material in this book was collected and how it was analysed, is that you will find yourself listening to children differently, with a better trained ear, encouraged to find ways to discover more about what they know and need to talk about.

Narratives and interpreting the transcripts

The branch of discourse analysis that underpins the way I worked with the transcripts explores the meanings, assumptions, feelings and emotional weight which seem to lie in the texts.

I start with the idea that narrative is at the heart of communication and learning. A number of theorists (both within and outside the world of education) have emphasised the importance of narrative for organising and making sense of one's experience, for exemplifying and communicating one's understanding of abstract concepts, and for making the connections between new ideas and what one already knows (for example Jerome Bruner, 1991, Mark Freeman, 1993). Narrative is also at the heart of the construction of identity. The stories we tell are 'who we are'. They hold the meanings of our experiences, the judgements we make. The children were continually breaking into stories to explain something to me, or because they were reminded of something they already knew that seemed relevant. I have tended to provide fairly long extracts from the transcripts to give you a flavour of these narratives. Some of the children were somewhat inarticulate or made grammatical mistakes, but I have not tried to correct their speech. Mediation through extracting and lifting material from its context is inevitable, but I want you to hear the children speak, even if it means that, like me, you sometimes have difficulty interpreting their meanings.

In listening to the narratives and trying to interpret them, I have needed to go beyond the overt information and listen for the emotional resonance, the underpinning values, beliefs, fears, anxieties that the words and the stories carry. This is something we all do when we communicate. We use cues of body language, tone of voice; we note what is quickly brushed over, where people trail off and don't complete a sentence, where they interrupt in their excitement, talk over other people, or seem to be talking in harmony, completing each other's sentences as if their thinking is happening in unison.

I have also been able to use the transcripts to consider children's talk over a long period and see where they have picked up an idea introduced by their partner much earlier in the interview, or returned to a theme. I have been able to look at the ways they fumbled for the words to express themselves, seem to find a fluent voice, often using the very phrases used earlier by their partner – or me. Sometimes you feel you can hear an adult authority somewhere else, speaking through the child. Children sometimes tell you that this is what their older sister, or their Gran or their Imam has said. Sometimes they don't, but the words have the familiar ring of community-held knowledge. This is one of the ways we all learn – to take on the 'script' from more experienced and respected people, which carries values and knowledge held in one's family and community.

Analysing transcripts

Analysing transcripts provides other opportunities to understand children's thinking. You can see how they seem to struggle with certain issues and sometimes misunderstand the question. The transcripts are full of examples of children's linguistic misunderstandings – particularly where they interpret language literally and fail to appreciate its metaphorical use. Several children said 'when grown-ups use long words we don't understand, but if they use shorter words we do'. Children regularly revealed that they did understand a concept when it was rephrased using familiar stories and easier language. Assuming that the ideas were beyond their understanding was a mistake. However, some children really didn't understand what I was asking them, ignored me and imposed their own agenda, which was illuminating about their understanding as well as their interests. Conceptual understanding was not necessarily age-related. Some insightful and sophisticated ideas came from the youngest children in the sample.

Looking for what is not there

Transcripts never tell you everything there is to know about a person. They are always the product of the particular context, the people who were present, the questions that were raised, the issues that were on someone's mind that day. However, interviews which go on for over an hour, picked up again on a different day and then followed up a week or more later, do provide positive evidence of persistent themes and attitudes.

When you are analysing transcripts, you should always look for what is left unspoken. Just because someone does not mention something does not mean she knows nothing about it or has no interest in it. People do not bother to mention what they take for granted. My interventions and probes were important not just in clarifying what children thought but also in finding out about something they had not introduced. Because it wasn't 'that' kind of research, I didn't follow up exactly the same issues with each pair of children.

At times one feels that children don't tell you something because they have chosen not to. You feel they know more than they give out, and sometimes this is confirmed because they decide to raise an issue later when presumably they feel more comfortable.

On the other hand, there are gaps in some transcripts that hit you between the eyes because virtually every other pair found the issues sufficiently important to talk about. This is where the middle-class children seemed to be living in a different social world to their working-class peers. They simply did not raise issues of crime, violence, child abuse and drugs. Some mentioned racism, but never as part of personal experience. They certainly wished 'people were nicer to each other' particularly in school, but the 'worst' story about antisocial behaviour offered by a middle-class child referred to people throwing sweet papers and crisp packets into their garden. This was in stark contrast to the experience and knowledge of violence – often linked with racism – explored in this book, and indicates the enormous gaps – created by social class – between children in the same year group in a school. Like many working-class children, they were concerned about the environment and about endangered species. But nowhere do you get an equivalent sense of concern with pressing social and emotional issues in their own immediate lives.

Who are the children in this book?

Altogether I interviewed 46 children from Years 3 to 6 in Mary Seacole and Sylvia Pankhurst Schools but I have drawn on the transcripts of only 34 children, since some of the material is repetitive or less relevant to the themes of this book. Some speak more poignantly than others. I will introduce the children in some detail, hoping you will feel you get to know them a little better as you read. Their personalities, interests and qualities become more multifaceted the more one listens to them and makes connections between different elements of their stories.

Ethnicities and class backgrounds

The official guidance from the QCA and in the National Curriculum assumes that questions of belonging, self-esteem and identity are uncontested, but we know that the heterogeneity of British society can lead to conflict and fractures in national identity.

Ethnicity	Nos.	Parents' ethnicity/countries of origin
African	3	Nigeria – Toyin, Edward Ghana – Akosua
African-Caribbean	4	Jamaica – Shakira Dominica/Jamaica – Jackie Jamaica/St.Vincent – Cherise St.Lucia – Janine
Bangladeshi	4	Bangladesh – Farzana, Abdul, Ibrahim, Naseem
Iraqi	1	Iraq – Mohamed
Of mixed-heritage* (mother shown first in the table of parental origin)	8	Italy/Turkish Cyprus – Leila Ireland/Turkish Cyprus – Gulsen Greek Cyprus /England – Harriet Zimbabwe-England/Jamaica – Francesca England/Portugal – Mena England/Jamaica – Simon (grandparents Poland/Scotland on mother's side; brother's father from Grenada) England/Ireland – Stephen (African-Caribbean grandfather) Dominica-England/ Tunisia – Ayshe
Moroccan	1	Morocco – Assia
White	13	Scotland – Rosalind, Angus, Sean England – Chrissy, Linda, Terry, John, Derek, Jo, England/Wales – Emily England/Scotland – Billy, Alex, Nicholas
	34	

The table above shows the ethnic backgrounds of the 34 children. The information comes from the children themselves. It also indicates the complex ethnic inter-relationships which increasingly characterise children in inner city schools and permeate their consciousness about race and identity. Some children who identified themselves as white had cousins who were black. Most children of ethnic minority heritage were born in Britain and so were some of their parents. Some volunteered information about grandparents, which I have included. Many children told me they spoke English at home and not their parents' mother tongue, though they could generally understand and converse in it with the older generation.

Schools, year groups and friendship pairs for the interviews

	Mary Seacole	*Sylvia Pankhurst*	*Nos.*	*Girls*	*Boys*
Year 3	Alex and Nicholas Gulsen and Akosua	Mohamed and Angus	6	2	4
Year 4	Billy and Stephen Emily and Harriet Jo and Derek	Toyin and Farzana Assia and Sean	10	5	5
Year 5	John and Terry Shakira and Linda	Abdul and Edward Rosalind and Naseem Janine and Ayshe	10	6	4
Year 6	Cherise and Francesca Chrissy and Leila	Jackie and Mena Simon and Ibrahim	8	6	2
Totals			34	19	15

Ethnicity and social class of the children in the book

	Ethnic minority, including of mixed parentage	White
Working-class	20	10
Middle-class	1	3

All these relationships pointed to personal, political and economic connections with a wider world, for white, local-origin children as well as those from ethnic minorities, and identification with people and places beyond this island's shores. This empirical evidence about the 'multiple identities' which underpin personal and national identities is of immense relevance to debates about identity and citizenship.

The Year 3 children

Alex (7yrs 4months) and Nicholas (7years 7months) Mary Seacole School

Both lived in large single-family, semi-detached Victorian houses near the school. Nicholas' father and mother were respectively artist/sculptor and printer. Alex's mother was an architect and his father a journalist. The youngest of four boys in his family, Alex generally answered sensibly and thoughtfully but he also used any opportunities to talk about fighting and war, to play-act bombing and planes with zooming and 'kabooming' sound effects. Nicholas did not join in this play. He had a sophisticated vocabulary and a wide general knowledge. He said his main interest in life was books and claimed to read some of his favourite books 'all night'. As well as some familiarity with current affairs in such places as Bosnia and Northern Ireland from watching the news on television, Nicholas knew something about the American Civil War and the Viking invasion of Britain, from his encyclopaedia at home. He talked about Nazi extermination policies of anyone who was not blue-eyed and blonde, though this had not been on the school curriculum. Nicholas had a full cultural life outside school, with holidays in Europe and the UK. He recalled in considerable and accurate detail what he had seen on visits with his father to the Natural History Museum and the Imperial War Museum. He told me about his father's zany sense of humour and activities such as looking for fossils on holiday in Ireland. Nicholas hoped to be a naturalist, a geologist and a meteorologist when he grew up.

Gulsen (7 years 2 months) and Akosua (7 years 7 months)
Mary Seacole School
Both lived in flats near the school but not the Seacole Estate. For both there was an issue of space in the home and a desire for privacy from younger and older siblings, and some way of being apart from adults. Gulsen's father was a cab driver, Turkish Cypriot in origin, and her mother was from Ireland. Gulsen provided a fascinating example of a multicultural upbringing. At weekends she went to Turkish school but also to church with her mother. She learned about 'Almighty God', miracles and 'the miracle of life' at Sunday School, where her mother was a teacher, but thought it was perfectly alright to believe in Allah and Islam as well. Gulsen knew there had been a war in Cyprus and had a distinctly Turkish perspective on the troubles, in which Greeks were the baddies and Turks the victims.

Both Akosua's parents came from Ghana and at home she sometimes spoke Twi as well as English. The importance of her Ghanaian connections and identity came through in a variety of ways. She had been to Ghana and told a story about her Ghanaian relatives' poor treatment at the hands of the police and the local community when they came to England. Akosua's home life seemed difficult. She talked about people in her family being angry and shouting, about being smacked and sent to bed without supper. Her father had left her mother and the children, gone off with another woman and then returned to Ghana. He was not in contact and in response to Gulsen's suggestion that she phone him, she said she did not have the number. Akosua knew about the civil war in Ghana because an uncle had been involved and she had watched news broadcasts about American involvement in Bosnia.

Mohamed (8 yrs 3 months) and Angus (8 yrs 4 months)
Sylvia Pankhurst School
Both lived on the Pankhurst estate. Mohamed's father was from Iraq, his family Muslim; Angus's parents were both white English and Christian. Both boys were chatty and uninhibited, with a fair amount to say about religion, drugs, the poor environment. Mohamed was deeply committed to Islam. Angus was unusual in talking about a good friend – a girl – who, he explained, was not his girlfriend but a 'real' friend.

The Year 4 children

Billy (8 years 11 months) and Stephen (8 years 8 months)
Mary Seacole School
Billy is white and Stephen of mixed heritage through a black grandfather. Billy's father was Scottish and his mum English, but he had cousins who were black. Billy shared his bedroom with his elder brothers. Stephen's 'original dad' was from Ireland, his step-dad Scottish, and his mum English. Stephen shared a room with two sisters, one a baby. Billy lived on the Seacole estate and Stephen in part of a house in a nearby main road but would have loved to live on the estate near Billy, because, he explained, his road was full of rubbish, there was a lot of crime and nowhere to play. However, Billy was not enamoured of the estate and complained of bullying and gangs. Both boys spoke about racism, fights in and out of school and unfair behaviour by adults such as supply teachers. Stephen was concerned about men and women fighting each other. Both had been out of London with their parents, Billy to Brighton and Blackpool, and Stephen to Portugal.

Emily (9 years) and Harriet (9 yrs 1 month) Mary Seacole School
Emily's parents were white English and Welsh, Harriet's father English and her mother Greek Cypriot. Both lived in single-family occupation houses in middle-class roads near the school. Harriet went to gymnastics and drama clubs and Emily studied gymnastics, ballet and flute out of school. Both had older siblings but each had her own bedroom. The girls had stories about nastiness at school, and how they tried sometimes to stop it but mostly didn't like to intervene. Harriet was concerned about racism. They were worried that little children might see unsuitable material on television and not realise when it was 'fake'. They wanted to be protected by adults from unpleasant issues such as the war in Bosnia. Both were concerned about endangered species and put this near the top of their list of important things, though they thought family and friends came above that. They were involved in setting up a cake stall to make money for a charity in Africa. Harriet had been on safari in South Africa with her parents when her father was on sabbatical.

Jo (8 yrs 9 months) and Derek (8 yrs 9 months)
Mary Seacole School
Jo is white, both his parents English. He lived on a Peabody Estate, about which he was positive and enthusiastic. Derek is also white and lived on a small council estate near the school, not the Seacole. His parents were both English but his aunt was Irish. Derek and Jo seemed easy-going characters, whose strategy for staying out of trouble was not to worry about fights if they weren't involved in them, to fight back if they needed to, to run if their opponents were bigger. Both Derek and Jo had experienced verbal abuse against their parents, who were not married, and this made them angry and unhappy. Both put their family at the top of the list of importance. Derek mentioned music and sport, and Jo was concerned about the fate of big cats. Jo had quite definite views and talked about political leaders and their political programmes, which he said he had learned about from his parents.

Toyin (8 years 8 months) and Farzana (9 years 2 months)
Sylvia Pankhurst School
Toyin's parents were both from Nigeria; she had been born there and came to England when she was 2. She lived near the Pankhurst

Estate. Her father had returned to Nigeria and she was uncertain when he would come back. Her mother sometimes spoke Yoruba but Toyin and her older sister mostly spoke English at home. Toyin talked at length about the unreliability of friends who manipulated and ganged up on her. Farzana's parents were both from Bangladesh but she was born in England, one of seven children. They were very cramped in a flat on the Pankhurst Estate. Both girls had experienced racism, including from African-Caribbean people. They were very interested in their respective religions (Christianity and Islam) and both put God at the top of their list of important things.

Assia (9 yrs) and Sean (8 yrs 4 months) Sylvia Pankhurst School
Assia was born in England but both her parents were Moroccan. Neither was in paid work. She spoke English with her siblings and Arabic with her parents. Assia was a feisty character who would give as good as she got, encouraged by her mother to fight back against any bullying or racism using karate. Sean's parents were Scottish and he had recently come from Sunderland 'because of trouble'. His father still lived up North. His mum was in work but his mum's Irish boyfriend was not. The transcript suggests that violence was part of life for both children, though not necessarily within the family. Sean was concerned about homelessness and poverty and had a non-judgemental attitude, feeling that one could explain what had happened to people through their bad luck in life.

The Year 5 children

Abdul (9 years 7 months) and Edward (9 years 8 months) Sylvia Pankhurst School
Abdul's parents were from Bangladesh and Edward's parents from Nigeria but both boys were born in England. Both lived on the Pankhurst Estate. There were seven children in Edward's family and his father was unemployed. Abdul had brothers and sisters but did not tell me whether his parents had paid work. Edward and Abdul's transcript has many references to fights – in school, between siblings and with other boys outside the school. Both were concerned about international violence, which they knew about from television. Abdul and Edward were the only children who openly asked about sex.

Rosalind (9 years 8 months) and Naseem (10 years)
Sylvia Pankhurst School
Rosalind identified herself as Scottish and she visited Scotland regularly to see her relatives. Her mother had remarried and there were no other children at home. Rosalind was one of the most powerful exponents of antiracism in the sample, inclined to deliver tirades against racists for their stupidity. Naseem was born in England but both her parents were from a small village in Bangladesh and her father returned quite regularly. She herself had visited once. Naseem's mother did not speak English. Naseem had some disturbing stories about the racist attacks suffered by her family on the Pankhurst Estate.

John and Terry (9 years 10 months) Mary Seacole School
Terry and John did not live on the Seacole Estate but in flats some way from the school. Both their parents were white English. Concern and love for their families comes through as the most important theme of their interview.

Shakira (9 years 10 months) and Linda (10 years 2 months)
Mary Seacole School
Shakira's parents had been born in England but her grandparents on both sides came from Jamaica. She lived on the Seacole Estate. Linda's family were white English on both sides. She lived in a block of flats near the school. Both talked about the violence on the Seacole Estate and the drug abuse. Linda's contribution to the transcript is notable for the level of guilt she felt about other people's difficult lives.

Leila (10 years 2 months) and Chrissy (10 years 7 months)
Mary Seacole School
Both girls lived on the Seacole Estate. Chrissy described her family as English. Leila's mother was Italian and her father Turkish Cypriot. The children spoke English at home, though Leila could understand and speak some Italian and some Turkish. Like other children with Turkish connections, Leila was aware of the historical conflict in Cyprus between Greeks and Turks. There had been a possibility that her father would get 'called' to go and fight in Cyprus and Leila had been extremely worried about this.

Janine (9 years 3 months) and Ayshe (9 years 3 months)
Sylvia Pankhurst School
Janine lived with her French-speaking mother who came from St Lucia and her older sister. She 'mostly' spoke English at home. Her father had left and she did not see him. The headteacher of Sylvia Pankhurst school told me that Janine's mother had had to be sectioned shortly before I did the interviews but was well at the time. Ayshe's parents had also split up. Her mother, an African-Caribbean/white woman, was from 'up north' and her father from Tunisia.

The Year 6 children

Ibrahim (11 years 2 months) and Simon (10 years 11 months)
Sylvia Pankhurst School
Ibrahim's family was from Bangladesh. His was a large extended family, with some members still in Bangladesh, whom the English side of the family visited. His family owned their own home near the school. Ibrahim asked me to note that he spoke Bengali, not Sylheti. He was extremely popular in his class and several children told me that he was a good friend. He spoke rapidly and confidently and seemed one of the most mature children in the whole sample. Ibrahim was particularly articulate about racism. Simon described himself as 'quarter caste', explaining that on his mother's side he was partly Scottish, partly Polish, and on his father's partly Jamaican. His brother's father was Grenadan. Simon was much quieter and more reserved than Ibrahim and initially withheld personal information, though he later talked about some of the difficulties in his family, including violence between his parents, drug abuse by a near relative who shop-lifted to support her habit and episodes with the law. Both boys had strong views about international religious conflicts, which they knew about from television.

Jackie (11 years) and Mena (11 years 1 month)
Sylvia Pankhurst School
Jackie lived on the Pankhurst Estate with her Dominican mother, Jamaican father and several siblings. She had a large extended family living nearby and was extremely close to her grandmother. Jackie was very knowing about some of the more antisocial activities on the estate such as drug abuse, theft and fencing, in which

members of her family had been involved. She was non-committal about this, though, like Mena, the muggings concerned her. Mena had been brought up by her English grandmother for her first five years, but now lived with her English mother and Portuguese father. Mena had things to say about the elderly victims of muggings.

Francesca (10 years 7 months) and Cherise (10 years 10 months) Mary Seacole School
Cherise lived on the Seacole Estate with her disabled mother, who was Jamaican. Her father, who came from St Vincent, had left them for another woman when Cherise was very young. Cherise was a very articulate, lively person, with many interests out of school. She was her mother's biggest fan, and described outings and visits that they made together, to museums and so on. Her friend Francesca was much quieter and more reserved. Both her parents were themselves of mixed parentage. Her maternal grandfather was from Zimbabwe, her father Jamaican/white English. Francesca and Cherise raised issues about teenage pregnancy and prostitution in the interviews.

2

Self-esteem, the family and respect

Sticks and stones can break your bones but words can never hurt you. It's not true. It's not a useful saying. You get hurt. Rosalind aged 9

This chapter starts with the familiar idea that high self-esteem connects with security and love within the family. But this is just to lay the ground for a discussion about how children wound, abuse and undermine each other by attacking their families. The PSHE and citizenship guidance advocates developing confidence in oneself, good relationships and respect towards others. The ability to withstand abuse and to refrain from using it against others is, at least in part, dependent on self-confidence and self-esteem. None of the children in this book had severe emotional difficulties but, typically, their lives were affected by the tensions of the inner city, particularly racism. Self-confidence and self-esteem develop with relation to the world in which the children are growing up, a world beset by serious inequalities and difficulties. It is not just that children have to negotiate and come to terms with these difficulties in their own lives, but that they also provide the ammunition which they can use against each other so effectively.

Self-esteem is sometimes considered a simple matter of individual characteristics which can be built up or undermined, for example through a teacher praising one's work, or someone disparaging one's prowess at sport. However, the literature emphasises that self-esteem is developed through a complex network of interactions and value judgements, in which the value one places oneself on the characteristic at issue, and also the significance of the person who is making the negative or positive judgement, all play their part. What comes through loud and clear from the transcripts of these KS2 children is how self-esteem is embedded in a sense of oneself as part of a functioning family, itself accepted and part of its community. School and the peer group are not irrelevant, but form one part of a tight triangle of relationships. All the more reason for school to establish relationships with families and communities, not to judge but to work with them.

'I'm OK, you're OK': Self-esteem and self-confidence

Developing high self-esteem underpins the guidance for PSHE/ citizenship education for KS 1 and 2. The rationale is not just to produce happy individuals but is grounded in generally accepted theories about the links between self-esteem, social behaviour and the ability to learn effectively. One does not need to be a therapist to accept that liking oneself is essential for being able to make and keep friends. Toleration and acceptance of others, whether or not they are intimate friends or acquaintances, is also theoretically based on self-acceptance and self-understanding. Most people who work with children whose emotional and behavioural needs have led to anti-social or self-destructive behaviour spend time building up their damaged and deflated sense of self. Sensitive teachers know from experience that low-self-esteem is often part of the problem for children who present difficulties settling effectively to their class work or getting on with their peers.

In Britain, much curriculum material developed for PSHE starts from the premise that high self-esteem is correlated with success in academic or social areas of school life and circle time and the approaches of emotional literacy are both intended to build up children's sense of self-worth and enhance tolerance. Research evidence from South Africa (Dean 2001) confirms the necessity to address respect for others. It demonstrates how, until the teacher recognised how far social and economic issues in the world outside the classroom were affecting her pupils' self-esteem and adopted a programme of circle time activities explicitly designed to address these issues, her pupils hijacked her objectives of collaborative learning and discussion. The first evaluations of Project Charlie, the anti-drugs project for Primary Schools in England, show that high self-esteem is correlated with the ability to resist negative peer pressure, and provide further evidence about the importance of high self-esteem.

It was never part of my research to test or score children on various aspects of self-esteem and correlate the results with such factors as ethnicity, economic and social status, or academic achievement. But during the interviews many children volunteered narratives about themselves and their peers which provided direct insights into their own understandings about the relationship between self-esteem and family life.

Learning to respect people

From the youngest child I interviewed to the oldest, the family was their source of security, values and identity. Parents – generally mothers in the case of girls and fathers and brothers for many boys – were their defenders in times of trouble, their positive role models and their valued advisers in difficult situations, noted and remembered in detail. Using language reminiscent of Abraham Maslow's (1968) hierarchy of needs – which they could not have known about – children saw their families as the source of their very life and continued existence. John (Y5), not normally very articulate, asked his own question at the end of the interview: 'do you like your family, why do you like your family and all that kind of stuff?' and answered: 'because I was born with them. I'm part of them and my mum and dad, they were the ones that made me, and if they weren't there I wouldn't be here, and if their mum and dad wouldn't have made them they wouldn't have been able to make me and my brothers, and my brothers wouldn't be able to make their children.'

Mutual respect played a central role in families seen as happy and successful. Given our concern with children learning to respect one another, the children's reasons for and examples of respect are illuminating. Eight-year old Mohamed greatly admired his father and grandfather. He told me what a good man his granddad had been: he didn't get angry, he didn't shout at his children. Mohamed had inferred lessons from within his family about respect. He did not respect grown-ups when they were 'rude'. 'Our family is not rude. But they are very happy,' he said. His friend Angus said, ' I just like the way I am. I'm normal. I don't like it if someone's not normal, a bit sick in the mind, like they're going to kill someone.' In poignant language, he linked being OK and living in a safe and happy family: 'I live peacefully and gratefully,' he said. 'I like the way we live, we just live nice and talk to each other nicely, we're a nice family. In my family, I worry about my family [meaning I care and feel concern for them] because they respect me and I respect them.' He contrasted the difficulty he might have if he had been adopted into another family. 'I wouldn't respect them. I would want to go back to my old family and they're like strangers when you first meet them. Even when I get used to them I still wouldn't respect them, because they're not my real family.' However, an adoptive family could redeem the situation by 'acting like my real family, like sometimes stories at bedtime and play with me'. For Shakira and Leila (Y5), respectful, caring relationships were based not on fear but on 'looking out for other people' and 'not answering back to your mum and dad'. They appreciated and respected their family members because they were kind to people, like Shakira's Grandad, who had 'offered a lift to an old man, in his van'. Leila's mum showed her care and concern by sticking up for her when Leila had trouble with children on the estate swearing at her and her sisters.

Cherise (Y6) contextualised her feeling that she was OK in her family relationships, particularly with her mother. Putting herself 'number one' in the list of what she thought important, she made direct connections between 'self-love' and the ability to love others. She thought her godfather had become obsessive about his job and lost sight of what was really important. 'The most important thing in life is you, your parents and the things you do ... you have to love yourself before you can love another person ... I learned that because my godmother and my godfather were married to one another, and he, instead of loving his self and his wife, he loved his job ... I've never seen my godfather again, he left my granny, he left ... he put too much love into his job... he could have, he could have loved my godmother.' Although Cherise deeply regretted not having a live-in father and at least one sibling – 'a four-person family all living together' – her unsolicited fanfare for her mother is one of the joys of the transcripts. 'I would like to be asked what's your mum like, is she like friends, does she do things with you, and do you go to exhibits and museums and go out to theatres?' she said. 'My mum's a Capricorn, a very friendly person, and even if you don't even know my mum you're sitting on a 38 bus or a 73 bus, and somebody gets on the bus, really weird or something, my mum can't sit there and be really tough facing the angry person. She'll say you can't always look on the bad things of life. That's what my mum is like. She's a very nice person, and I wish everybody was like my mum, and when I grow up I'd like to be exactly like my mum, a couple of changes, but just like my mum.' It is not hard to infer that Cherise's self-confidence relates at least in part to this strong identification with a mother she so admires and loves.

In a memorable statement, Terry (Y5) explained that nothing, and certainly not money, was as important as love and the family: 'You love all your family and the important things are your heart and your family and that's what I think about all their hearts in the family.' Neither he nor his friend John wanted to change anything about themselves or their families.

When I asked Mena and Jackie (Y6) if they wanted to change anything about themselves, they both laughed. Mena answered, 'No, I'll be like I am now,' and Jackie said 'Yeh'. Though Mena was liable to be smacked by both her parents (which she mentioned more than once) she felt very secure in her immediate family; she put family at the top of her list of importance 'because they cared for me, they reared me, they gave me clothes and food and everything. Especially my Granny,' Mena added, 'because she reared me for five years, and she never says no to me, and if my dad ... if I get smacked, she says OK, don't cry.'

Jackie also put her family top of her list. 'They're the ones that look after you, you should have some respect for them, they put clothes on you and food in your mouth.' Like Mena, her Granny had a special place. 'Especially my Granny ... cos like every Sunday, like she works right through the day, she doesn't work for someone else, she makes things, she puts them in the two shops that's really close to her, and she has to look after, um fifteen people in one household, yeh, that are all in the one house... and every Sunday we get our bacon and eggs.'

The sad, the worried and the guilty

If some children were openly positive about themselves, others seemed sad, worried or guilty. Since I did not rigorously check out my hunches about the relationship between self-esteem and family life I can offer only tentative inferences from their responses, particularly to the question 'what makes you sad or angry'. Some children said directly that they felt ashamed of their own behaviour and talked about guilt, or they used a discourse of powerlessness and helplessness. However, one needs to guard against an unrealistic view of how much power children might expect to have. As many before me have noted and the children themselves were quick to point out, lack of power in an adult world is virtually a definition of childhood in contemporary Britain.

Naseem and Rosalind (Y5) were interesting characters. Considered 'stars of the show' by their teacher, their interviews were characterised by dramatic acting out of strongly held views. One might have thought both were children with high self-esteem and confidence. However, careful listening and giving them space to take a lead in the content of the interview allowed a more nuanced impression, and suggested that there were important differences between the two. Both thought that 'acting rude and trying to be cool' was 'ridiculous'. They distanced themselves from such behaviour, chorusing together 'we're sensible.' Rosalind continued, with Naseem occasionally butting in to agree: 'I think for myself. I just say, I'm sorry, but that is not cool. Helping people, being smart, being nice to people, that's cool.' When they were talking about racism, Naseem said that when people abused her about her family, she retorted, 'I like the way they are, it's *my* family, they don't have to change the way *you* want them.' Rosalind mentioned that her parents had split up before she was born and then came back together again, an issue which seemed to be on her mind, and Naseem offered, 'My dad and mum love each other so much, they wouldn't split up.'

During the interview Rosalind became overexcited and heated, shouting and acting out other children's 'stupid' behaviour in a mocking, exaggerated voice. 'They only have half a brain', she cried repeatedly. She said firmly that she was quite capable of sorting things out for herself if there was trouble. But another section of the interview suggested that a frightened little girl lurked behind the bravado, 'scared of going upstairs at night to get [her] pyjamas, scared that someone was hiding in the house who might come and grab you, scared that you might end up on the streets, because your mum and dad are getting in huge arguments, so you get scared and you run away, and you say I can't go back because they might not be living there.'

I have little doubt about Rosalind's principled and strongly-held views about justice and racism (which you'll find in Chapter 3). But might the off-putting, confrontational bombast undermine her effectiveness as a committed, concerned citizen who might actually change things? This is where I believe genuine self-confidence and commitment come together. To help Rosalind become a more effective citizen, one would have to take on her inappropriate methods of dealing with differences between people and help her towards a more tolerant and insightful approach which would lead to better strategies. This might begin with awareness of the underlying insecurity in some of Rosalind's outward behaviour.

Simon told a story against himself. He was ashamed that he had turned on his little brother when his frustration was actually against his mother for stopping him from watching telly. 'I feel sad if I hurt my brother. Straightaway I felt more angry because I'd hit him and he'd got me in trouble, but I didn't hit him again, but I felt sad because I'd hit him.' Simon had another story which suggested that he understood the connection between personal insecurity and 'hard' antisocial behaviour: 'Some of my family concern me. My aunt was put in gaol... She was stealing from handbags. I'm concerned about my cousins, her kids, they act all hard. I don't want to turn out like that.' Early in the interview Simon said there were 'private things' about his family that he did not want to talk about. Later, when he relaxed with me, he said 'it makes me sad if my dad hits my mum or something'.

Both Ibrahim and Simon felt it was important to have the 'guts' to challenge bullying or threatening behaviour. Ibrahim made clear links between 'guts', the courage of one's convictions, and intervention in antisocial or even illegal behaviour. Understandably, although he 'did not have the guts' to do something about a man he knew who wasted his money and whose children didn't have enough food, he had stood up for his cousin who was getting bullied and wouldn't tell anyone. 'I couldn't take it any more', he explained, so he had told his mum knowing that the situation would then be resolved. In contrast, Simon confessed to feelings of powerlessness. 'I feel I have to say something but I don't have the guts,' he said. 'The babysitter hits me with a stick.' He acknowledged that Ibrahim's advice 'to run upstairs to phone his aunty or the police' was sensible, but he preferred not to involve his mum, though he did not explain why.

Edward and Abdul (Y5) offered chilling information about the extent they or their siblings would go when upset. Abdul observed, 'I like life because you can enjoy yourself. But sometimes when my mum or dad hits me I say I want to die. I don't really. And sometimes you can injure yourself and sometimes when I get into a fight I pick up a knife to injure myself.' I asked whether this was really a bluff, to frighten the other person, and Abdul answered, 'Yes, they won't hit me no more.' Edward picked up the theme of self-mutilation. 'My sister says she wants to kill herself and she just scratches herself, but when she's thinking about it she wishes she never did it'.

Guilt about other people's pain or hurt feelings was a theme running through the interview with Leila and Chrissy (Y6). Very early on, Leila spoke of feeling guilty about being embarrassed that her mum walked with her to school. She confessed, 'I can't tell my mum. I can't actually say that to my mum because I feel guilty... I feel really guilty and ashamed of myself and everything.' It turned out, however, that guilty feelings were not completely negative since for both girls they also involved compassion and led to attempts to intervene on others' behalf. Although Chrissie personally didn't say racist things, she felt guilty about other people who did. 'Say like when someone's beating someone then I... when I see them beating up I feel guilty for them, I try not to... well normally we help them, sort of like we hold them back... I just feel guilty about it, I try not to feel guilty. I just feel funny inside.' I asked if she sometimes simply walked away and she answered, 'Well yea I do, but like, when I walk away, I just ... it's in my head.' Leila continued, 'What I do when I feel guilty about people, or when I feel guilty, yea, because Shazia just got beaten up, then what I do is I go over to them and I keep them company and things like that, and I would be nice to them, and I wouldn't ignore them.'

Near the end of the interview Chrissy returned to the theme and, as one of her own questions, asked to talk about why people feel guilty. Her answer came in a rush. 'I feel guilty because whenever people like say, people pick on people, I feel really really guilty and stuff, because I feel sorry for them, and I care, I care about it, really, all the people who have something wrong and people in hospital and things like that, blind people and things like that, that's me, why I feel guilty.'

These stories from Simon, Edward, Abdul and Chrissy give us pause for thought. Simon appears reasonably open but at first did not want to talk to me about family difficulties, though it emerged that Ibrahim already had some insight into his friend's personal life. This must be the case for many children: that what is happening in their home lives is linked with shame and guilt. In the context of what children had to say about open abuse of each other's families (reported later in this chapter), one can see that to make such personal information public is to open oneself up to potential exploitation. Teachers may be wholly unaware of the extent of the difficulties in some children's lives.

Verbal abuse, getting into fights and family loyalty

In the light of the importance of their family to the children's self-esteem, we look next at the prevalence of verbal abuse directed towards children's families and consider what this implies for citizenship education. Self-esteem rests on a secure identity and identity implies a sense of belonging and acceptance, not just by your primary carers but within a community. You cannot feel comfortable, secure and fully accepted when you and your family are subjected to abuse about your colour, religion, ethnicity or economic standing. Chapter 3 shows how racist abuse acquires its greatest power to hurt young children when it is channelled through abuse of the family. These are Human Rights issues. Simplistic *a priori* admonitions about what is 'right and wrong' don't hold up in the children's world. Many children have their own theories about antisocial behaviour and have already made decisions about what is right and wrong. They are often taking matters into their own hands through direct action, since they perceive that these transgressions merit retaliation. This creates a different set of problems for the school, since it is generally agreed that 'responsible and effective members of society' should not resort to violence.

Over and over again the children made it crystal clear that they are at their most vulnerable when members of their family are under attack and that fights regularly start because of well-honed and extremely effective techniques of personal abuse, particularly against mothers. Such abuse may or may not include racism, but its hallmark is aspersions cast against parents' ability to look after their children appropriately – to house, clothe or even feed them. Though sometimes the attacker would backtrack and claim to be 'only joking', deliberate and pointed abuse of the family demanded retaliation. It is hard to imagine anyone, adult or child, remaining unaffected by such deliberate insult to their family and their primary identity. Children understood the effects of these insults and themselves indulged in deliberate provocation. That they were sometimes the insulted and wounded victims did not mean that they would abstain from hurting others. The success of PSE and citizenship education must be evaluated in the wider context of the children's lives, not just within the school. Even if abuse and fighting is kept in check within the school, we need to acknowledge that our strategies do not appear to have credibility outside, where another ethic operates.

The ethic of self-defence and retaliation was actively encouraged by many parents, whose advice was respected over and above that of teachers. Children perceived their parents as having greater concern and knowledge about their lives, as effective in defending them against violence and bullying, and more likely to give advice that worked, while teachers neither intervened effectively nor stopped the bullying in the longer term. Time and again children complained that the rule to go and tell a teacher if there was trouble left them without defences and open to continued bullying. As John pointed out: 'In year 4 I used to get bullied by these boys and when I used to try and defend myself the whole class would come against me and jump on me... and they started to boot me in the head.' When I asked what happened then, John said, 'I told the teacher... and they just carried on they just go'ed on bullying me.' Then John told his parents ... 'and my dad he said give them a right whack, so I went to the school the next day and they kept on abusing me, so I gave a whack to one of them, and he never started on me again, but then the next time, it was just a couple of weeks ago, I gave him another whack, but I just keep getting into trouble... but they're not bullying me anymore. All I'm concerned is not being bullied.'

Some schools are challenged by the obscurity of the causes of the fighting that breaks out between children. Boys in particular explained that they were regularly in trouble because they came to the defence of friends or members of their extended families who were being physically abused or bullied. Girls as well as boys were open about fighting and discounted any idea that it can break out without provocation. Though very ready to lay the blame elsewhere, one can assume that many of the children who claimed to be innocent were guilty of provoking fights and not just on the receiving end.

The simple phrase 'your mam' as identified by Kelly (Kelly and Cohn 1989), spoken with a particular sneer, a jeering inflection, still rates among the most hurtful insults. When probed, children explained that the mother was being accused of lacking the female qualities of caring and providing for their children, of making a reasonable living, of being able to clothe their children from new and not second-hand shops. To push the point home, children would say 'your mum' (or dad) about some particularly broken-down person.

Jo and Derek (Y4) insisted on writing down rather than articulating the 'strong swear-words' used against their mums and dads. 'Your mum' or 'your dad' left it to the recipients to fill in their own imagined hurt. 'It's like they're calling your mum fat and ugly, or they say you're a bastard... that means you ain't got a dad'. I observed that actually bastard meant that someone's mum and dad weren't married. But I was off the mark. Illegitimacy was not the issue – the implied taunt was that fathers were absent or were not fully committed to their children. Both Jo and Derek quickly said that their parents weren't married, but 'that don't mean I'm a bastard' and anyway, their dads were around. They mentioned that children even called Terry, whose father had died, a bastard, and that this was particularly horrible. 'They want to make you feel bad, they wanna upset you, they just wanna make you cry. They just try until it does upset me.' Derek explained that though it was upsetting, 'it don't feel the same when they cuss my friends, because they're not as close as my mum and dad'.

Toyin said, 'I get in lots of fights. Sometimes people force you, get you mad, you try and ignore, but you can't... they say about your family, you can't afford to get a house... most of the time it's about your family. They call you... you're a pig, and your mum doesn't even wear proper clothes, you can't afford to buy things... If you walk down the street and you see this drunk man, or tramp, they'll go: that's your father. That tramp looks just like you, the clothes you're wearing.'

Linda told me, 'One of the girls said 'that's your mum' and then she said 'well your mum's a poof... your mum's gay. Well it just like concerns you and stuff, then cos they say things about your mum, and you get upset and then unless (sic) I'm really mad I say things about her mum. . . it hurts your feelings and then makes you angry. Like your mum's dead, or something like cancer or aids, or your mum's a poof, [and then] we'll fight.' The word 'gay' has been hijacked in the school community to insult without any necessary association with homosexuality (*TES*, 19.1.01). Linda knew that the word was being misused but it was still hurtful.

Like Jo and Derek, Rosalind and Naseem were adamant that swear-words were meant to hurt. The adage that stick and stones can break your bones and words can never hurt you was not true, Rosalind said with great vehemence. 'It's not a useful saying. You do get hurt.' Refusing to say the words that were used about them and their parents, they wrote 'cunt' and 'bitch' on my notebook. 'They go on about your family,' Rosalind explained. 'They bully your little sister and brother and they go up to your mum and your dad and your generation, your whole family.'[I interpret Rosalind to mean that younger children are bullied in person, and that the whole family, from youngest to oldest, is subject to open season for abuse.] Naseem mimicked the voice of children who insulted her, 'You're just like a dog. Your whole family's dogs. You've got so many dogs in your family you don't even know which one is your mum.'

Abdul said, 'these boys started cussing me. I was sad. They was bigger than me, round 15. Sometimes they say rude things. They were cussing my mum and about my culture.' Talking about 'cussing' reminded Edward that 'Elias cusses people who is poor. He saw a woman who had a cardigan with holes in, she had no shoes. She tied some cardigan on her feet, and he was cussing her.' Later I asked what made them angry or sad and Edward returned to the theme: 'if people cuss my family.' Abdul explained on his behalf, 'He gets really angry, because he doesn't like it.' Like Rosalind and Naseem, they refused to say the offending words but wrote a number of four letter sexual words on my notepad which included those conventionally used about prostitutes.

Jackie and Mena told me about Fauzia, a child in their class who was victimised. Jackie explained, 'I used to like give Fauzia clothes... her mum might not be poor, but she don't have that much money, so Fauzia don't have nice clothes and Sharon was picking on her.' Mena added, 'Also Fauzia was crying. People say things about your mum, and where you live.' Jackie completed the story, assuming three different voices, one for herself, one for the boy in the story and one for Fauzia. 'Well, cos I was sitting at the dinner table the other day, and this boy goes, 'I saw Fauzia kicking a tin can, and I said, what are you doing Fauzia' and she goes 'I'm moving house'. I didn't laugh in her face though, because it was sad.'

Beyond recognition of the pain it causes, there is great irony in the actual content of the abuse, where the very values of respectability promoted in wider society backfire. Though one middle-class girl, Rosie (not one of the children represented in this book) did talk about being bullied, it was significant that not a single one of the middle-class children mentioned suffering similar abuse. If my own children had come home saying we had been called idiots or tramps, I would certainly have wanted to deal with the emotional hurt they experienced. However, I would have had facts to support my comforting words that there was absolutely no truth in the accusations – our academic record, the clothes in our cupboards bought new, the furniture in our comfortable house. I would have argued that the abuse was not to be taken seriously and possibly reflected jealousy or resentment. The children who can be hurt by aspersions on their parents' ability to hold the family together, by references to absentee fathers or taunts that their mother is a whore, are living in communities on the margins, where, at least for some, there is a grain of truth in the accusations.

The statistics from the schools themselves and the evidence from the surrounding areas tell their own story. In both areas, the shops where everything costs £1 and the local charity shops are the size of warehouses, and are always full of people picking over the discarded toys, the shrunken, fluff-balled cardigans, the boots and shoes stretched to accommodate someone else's bunions. Over half the children in Sylvia Pankhurst and over a third in Mary Seacole were entitled to free school meals. Taunts that 'your mum's a tramp who can't afford to buy proper things' are particularly painful if you are growing up in a single-parent household headed by a woman who struggles daily to stay presentable and solvent with scant resources, or if both your parents are unemployed. Children whose parents were abused as 'tramps' or 'idiots' could not be comforted by their parents' A-levels, degree or secure job. For some children the insults were nowhere near the truth, but the implications of poverty and family inadequacy were nevertheless deeply hurtful, given the negative connotations in their own communities. For others, the words cut to the bone because there was a possible grain of truth.

The citizenship guidance has nothing to say about respecting difference or learning to live in an unequal society. From Aristotle to Parekh, commentators on society have noted that there cannot be genuine democracy in situations of social and economic inequality. The children's stories of abuse show yet another way in which the social hierarchy and economic inequalities undermine respectful behaviour between citizens. The powerful hegemonic value systems of the privileged and successful provide the language for children living on the run-down, dirty, crime-ridden estates to hurt each other, and voice harsh judgements of inadequacy, ironically misappropriating the language of 'family values' and economic viability.

As a historian I am reminded of the prevalence of 'respectability' as a value system among upwardly aspiring working people living on or below the bread-line in the nineteenth century and in pre-Second World War Britain. Women put their clothes in pawn and kept their children indoors when they didn't have shoes in which to send them to school but polished their front doorstep to maintain appearances. So I am not suggesting that schools are attempting to impose values which are separate from children's home lives, for it is clear that the values of respectability and solvency come from the family. Nevertheless, the situation is genuinely dilemmatic for teachers. On the one hand, you are expected to instil ideals of family security and economic viability which are the markers of successful citizenship. On the other, you may be aware of genuine misfortune, and know that children insult others and distance themselves from poverty or family difficulties. Many children were cynical about exhortations not to fight back or 'tell a teacher'. Such advice seems particularly feeble if the abuse continues outside the school, a no-go area for most teachers. It is not enough for the school to be a safe place for the few hours of the day when children are within its walls, if, like water closing over a stone, life reverts to a different and more violent reality when they leave at 3.30.

What can we do?

If our efforts to enhance self-esteem and mutual respect are to be realistic, relevant and lasting, we need to educate ourselves about children's actual experience and what they know and care about in their personal lives outside school. We are – rightly – concerned about confidentiality, about the boundaries between the public and private, about teachers' roles, which are neither that of personal therapists nor social workers. The ethical issues are complex. If we take PSHE seriously, we might find ourselves treading in extremely sensitive areas; we also have to report to parents on their children's progress in PSHE. The way forward may be to distinguish between sensitive personal information and the abusive language designed to hurt, starting with the emotional aspects and working with concepts of compassion, empathy and concern for others. I discuss such ideas further in Chapter 6. We might also consider the knowledge and understandings (or ignorance and misunderstandings!) that underpin these discourses, which I return to in Chapters 4 and 7.

Teachers can certainly use the open-ended conversational strategies I used. As I argue later with respect to bereavement, the first necessity is to acknowledge that what one knows may be the tip of the iceberg, and that one may never be in a position to elicit the evidence for one's hunches directly. The questions I asked to elicit feelings and understandings about self and family are not beyond the scope of circle time. I did not know the children better than their teachers do. Sensitivity and trust are paramount. Not all the material was confidential but children nevertheless told me that they were never asked about such matters. The interview procedure allowed them to pass over questions if they wanted to, and was sufficiently open-ended for them to be in control of what they said. It was perhaps more important that the interviews were not a public forum. Only a 'best friend' was present, and though the children knew the material would 'go further', their anonymity was assured. As I found in the pilot work, the composition of the group made all the difference to what children revealed. There are already classrooms where such trust and genuine exploration of emotions occurs. Plenaries are not compulsory for PSHE! Talented, mature teachers exist everywhere, who gradually build up trust so that children will come and talk to them on an individual level. Schools with high levels of economic and social disadvantage might want to consider having someone with the counselling skills and knowledge to help children directly or refer a child on.

Dealing with generalised abusive behaviour is different from exploring sensitive personal issues. In our inner city schools, some kind of safety net is needed but expectations about public disclosure may well be wrong. There is a variety of games and approaches which retain anonymity while still providing opportunities to express fears and emotions. This is the sphere of emotional literacy and circle time.

Insight as a strategy for positive intervention

Acquiring insight into their own and other children's behaviour and concentrating on the possibility of change are ways forward. This may mean challenging deterministic explanations held by several children, for instance that one couldn't expect anything different from children who were following the bad example of parents. John and Terry (Y5) jointly told a story of a bad boy who 'got barred' from school and various places on the estate. He had smashed a boy's head on the window and 'he was beating them up' but they reckoned he was copying his dad, who was a bully. 'Yeah, they want to copy their dad,' John declared. Stephen and Billy (Y4) had similar theories about a girl who was always fighting and swearing. They believed that antisocial behaviour ran in families, continuing through different generations: Billy started the story, which Stephen continued: 'Because her mum, ... most children want to be cool, but some other children just learn it from their mums. She gets bad behaviour off her mum, and *her* mum was probably bad, so Michelle's mum got her bad behaviour off *her* mum.' 'Then when Michelle's mum came up to the class, the teacher weren't in there, and she was swearing and everything at John, in front of the children, and now Michelle swears at everyone.'

Other children, however, took responsibility for their own behaviour, clearly believed in choice, and demonstrated a conscience or at least some rationalisation of their own poor behaviour, which could be a starting point for change and learning to consider each others' feelings. When Angus and Mohamed (Y3) moved up into the juniors, they decided to 'change themselves', 'change their style' as Mohamed put it. 'Like me and Angus, we were very naughty and we improved.' Angus explained: 'When people started to make trouble we said, we won't talk as well... everything's much better now... The kids say you've got better and you're not disturbing us.'

Toyin and Farzana (Y4) seemed to be drawing on a notion of a 'true and good self' which was sometimes overruled by circumstances beyond their control. They recognised the importance of being able to resist peer pressure, and explained that there are occasions when you go against your true nature because you are being forced or manipulated or there are divided loyalties. Toyin wished there were not so many fights in school. People became sad and angry, but it was not easy to stay out of them. Farzana explained: 'People make you fight. They say, go and fight with that person or I'm not your friend. They'll tell you what to do, but you'll end up crying. It's hard to say no. It's your friend and you can't say no to them.' Toyin agreed that 'sometimes you don't act like yourself, you act different, because you're around with your friends'.

Other children knew they shouldn't get into fights but were put in a double bind when their friends needed them to intervene. This is a telling example of how teachers can oversimplify morality with absolutes like 'don't fight'. Without wishing to promote a violent society ruled through strength and bullying, I find myself asking: 'What, never? Never stick up for your family or friends when they are being victimised or abused?'

Self-esteem and empathy

Tolerance and empathy imply understanding and accepting the context and the reasons why people do things the way they do and appreciating the feelings they may be experiencing. Some children were not just tolerant but proposed solutions to other children's problematic behaviour. Noticeably, the children who showed *personal* insight seemed to understand their peers. They were less likely to be judgemental, demand conformity and they were less deterministic. They recognised that tolerance and maturity, and especially the ability to walk away from trouble or not take things out on the nearest person, are connected to how one feels about oneself, one's sense of personal security and well-being. Francesca (Y6) talked about a girl who bullied others, 'not a person I can relate with'.

When I asked Francesca why the girl was like that, her answer was thoughtful: 'People say it's because of people's backgrounds. If you're troubled, something like that. I've been to her house twice and her mum is from Wales and she has a little brother, but not by the same dad, and it's like she doesn't really like her mum. It's got to do with having another dad. She said the man's really horrible, but when I went there, he was really nice... Sometimes if you don't feel loved ...'

Like several others, Linda and Shakira (Y5) explained some anti-social behaviour, which they called 'jealousy', in terms of resentment of someone's talents or good fortune. These talents would not be acknowledged and praised but undermined through personal name-calling, which often got the victim into trouble for retaliating. Trying to get at the root of this, I asked why children used hurtful language in the first place. Was it just a way of cussing those they didn't like? Linda explained how situations escalated. 'It's cos, cos like they might be jealous or something, and that's why, because sometimes they couldn't do things same as me, they weren't allowed to do some things, and then they would, they just say things about my mum, just to make me upset. But then like they've got you in trouble... if the teacher didn't even know what happened and she took one person's side they didn't do anything and then they made it even worse...' Shakira agreed. 'That's what happened to me... cos I go to gymnastics, we done gym and because they were seeing who could do the best one, I done the best one and then like they were giving me dirty looks and stuff and I said to them, there's no need to be jealous, it's only like a cartwheel or something... and then, then they just called me names.'

Jackie and Mena thought that Tony, about whom many children in Sylvia Pankhurst school complained, was the victim of scapegoating and unfair labelling, so he couldn't get recognition even when he was trying. They also felt that Tony 'who can be really bad' was seeking attention. They thought he was more sensitive than the teachers realised, and became terribly upset and cried if he was unfairly told off. There were also problems in his family. Tony did not love or respect his family, and this, Jackie suggested, could cause extreme insecurity in the child. 'They might just put you in a child home (sic) and go about their business...'

Ibrahim and Simon corroborated Jackie and Mena's comment that Tony was the victim of negative labelling by teachers. 'Sometimes the teacher won't let him have a chance to speak for himself, she'll go, just get inside to Mrs C. Like he'd been naughty before, he was crazy, but now he's much better. Just because he was bad before, everyone has to go 'well that's it.". Their theory about why Tony was trying to change himself is good news for teachers who decide to adopt a less punitive approach to challenging behaviour. Apparently they had relaxed their former zero-tolerance to Tony. Ibrahim said, 'I think it was the teachers, like first they was too hard on him, they gave him too much pressure and he couldn't take it.' Simon agreed, 'Yeh, they gave him too much pressure.' Ibrahim summed up, 'Yeh, too much pressure. And then when he's treated well by the teachers, then he behaves better. When the teachers are too hard on him, and don't let him speak for himself, unfair teachers, he can't cope with some teachers. Nearly all supply teachers, they shout for no reason, they pick on us for whispering.'

Jackie and Mena described a classmate, Clare, as mocking and bullying smaller weaker children, and doing stupid things like tearing up all the leaflets in the library and refusing to pick them up. They said she was 'trying to prove something'. 'What's the point,' Jackie commented, 'It doesn't prove much, does it?' Naseem and Rosalind, both high achievers who received much affirmation from teachers, thought that as well as seeking attention, some children who did not achieve praise for good work needed to build up their own image in public. They tried to be 'cool and act big and strong' or, like Andrew, a particularly challenging and unhappy boy, resorted to lies and pretence that the teacher had praised him, to gain positive attention from his peers.

Feminist-influenced approaches to ethics emphasise that justice and ethical behaviour are not just about knowing a variety of rules, 'understanding about' other people's practices, and then being in a position to make decisions about what to do, but demand qualities of empathy and care. The extract from Chrissy and Leila's interview on pages 32-33 may be at an extreme end of a continuum of concern for others, and I for one would be uneasy about fostering such guilt. Nevertheless, there is something in their transcript that deserves recognition, namely a capacity to empathise with other people and readiness to intervene to help them. Several children showed some appreciation that problems in their own or other people's lives might lie at the root of alienation and disaffection: Edward and Abdul talked about self-mutilation; Naseem and Rosalind acknowledged their peers' need for positive affirmation even as they mocked 'acting hard' and showing off as 'uncool'. And there were the four children in Tony's class who talked about how he was labelled by teachers. All had something to say about understanding antisocial behaviour and such discussion could be part of a managed class debate about what wounds us and why some of us hurt others.

If my analysis is correct, then encouraging empathy and personal tolerance will be only part of effective intervention strategy. That so many children perform verbal violence against one another using their parents' real or imagined economic insecurity as the weapon, suggests they have internalised the message that poverty or lack of work are individual failings. As the next two chapters show, ignorance and misunderstandings about society, as well as prejudice, are responsible for antisocial behaviour. The opportunity to gain knowledge to dispel the misconceptions, and the chance to explore and debate the nature of a just society are part of the solution.

The next chapter is devoted to an issue at the heart of children's lives in the inner city and fundamental to Citizenship education – racism.

3

Identity, racism and belonging

'It doesn't matter what religion you are, you're still a human being... you're not an alien from outer space.' Ibrahim (aged 11)

Racism damages vulnerable people's identification with the state and their sense of being an equal citizen, and it undermines democracy. A cursory review of twentieth century history confirms that it is contradictory and self-defeating to work towards democracy without tackling racism. So basic is its negative impact on citizenship that a curriculum which fails to take on the children's experience of racism is not worth the paper it's written on.

Racism has an immediate impact on one's sense of self. This can be psychologically destructive or it can lead to strong and active resistance, which may need to be constructively channelled. The majority of children I talked with came from ethnic minority communities; everyone was living and going to school in multicultural environments, and racism was inseparable from their lived experience. The majority of children introduced this issue themselves, sometimes with passion. In the light of prevalent racism, what might 'playing an active role as citizens' mean for the citizenship curriculum? The transcripts demonstrate the inadequacy of a so-called 'minimalist agenda' to prepare them helpfully for their future.

Identity, acceptance and belonging may be central to a healthy citizenry but pride in one's personal identity is not always confirmed by others; they may use the very aspects of your personal identity which are most important to you to 'diss' you and your family. The ethnic minority intake was 80% in Sylvia Pankhurst and 27% in

Mary Seacole, but neither school had a majority of children of Caribbean or South Asian origin (the main ethnic minority groups in Britain, along with Irish). Though the children in my research may not represent the majority in the country as a whole, or the actual proportions of different ethnic groups in the population, the 'numbers game' is irrelevant when we talk about human rights and identity.

The children did not use the word 'identity', and they did not complain of racist abuse within the school context. Most were appreciative and respectful of their teachers (though supply teachers did not fare so well). But neither school really addressed the lives of the children outside of school, their concern about feeling safe and belonging in the community. Some, though not all, perpetrators of abuse outside the school boundaries were current pupils and older youths who were ex-pupils. The challenge for schools is not so much what to do within school, where the rules may be very clear and effectively enforced and where the children feel relatively safe. It is rather an issue of the 'staying power' of the values of citizenship within the broader community.

I believe that a citizenship curriculum should educate children to understand how racism undermines human rights and democracy, going beyond personalised explanations which concentrate on individual nastiness and helping children develop strategies to challenge and resist.

Some children provided an unexpected, unsettling perspective on Parekh's (2000) notion of a 'community of communities', with its cosy, welcoming and protective connotations. In fact, within the community of the big estates, which may appear relatively homogenous to people who don't live there, compared to the streets and communities outside, several smaller communities were attempting to co-exist, with varying degrees of success. The lines of fracture of these mini-communities seemed to be along ethnic and religious lines, reproducing in microcosm the prejudices and pressures of wider society. Children of South Asian heritage, and children perceived to be Muslim even if they were not, were most at risk.

High self-esteem and wider aspects of identity

All the literature on social inclusion recognises that 'identity' is not just a set of individual psychological characteristics related to one's interests, abilities and character, developing in the context of family alone or the small world of school. Positive identities do not develop in a social vacuum but are sustained or undermined through positive or negative experiences in the wider political, economic and social arena. Children growing up in communities with long-term unemployment may have difficulty escaping from a prevailing culture of cynicism about their prospects, which will affect their identification with mainstream values. Families who are aware and articulate about the discrimination they suffer will pass on such values to their children, who may judge and potentially reject what the school has to offer and identify with resistance rather than conformity. There are implications for national identity: to be repeatedly told that your ways of doing things are not accepted and that you, and people like you, don't belong in the place that you regard as home, is undermining and destructive.

David Smail, a clinical psychologist and psychotherapist working in the NHS, has explored how living in a pathological social world can lead to feeling out of control of one's life, generating debilitating emotional distress (Smail, 1993). This has particular relevance to both institutionalised and street racism and it moves the debate away from individualised incidents. Smail acknowledged that although interventions and 'treatments' for such social pathology were seldom possible for any individual, people benefited from explanations which contextualised and made sense of their difficulties in a wider landscape. Over and above the advantages of 'talk therapy' in the case of racism, both white and black pupils can be preparing themselves for actively changing the nature of their society in due course, but only if they have a framework which goes beyond individualised cases.

The damage done by racism goes wide and deep. Since, as the children's transcripts unequivocally show, abuse of the family is regularly and typically part of racist abuse, ethnic minority children are subjected to doubly painful rejection: of themselves for who they are, and of the families they feel part of.

Toyin and Farzana told me about a family whose home was vandalised while they were in Bangladesh. 'The news goes everywhere. Sofas cut in half, television robbed,' Farzana mused. Farzana's own family had experienced vicious racism. 'English people cuss you about your religion and try and rob your friends... They cuss you and say 'everybody's scared of me' and cuss you and say things like wash your hair, you've got bad dandruff... and your eyes and them stuff.' I asked what she meant by 'English'. She replied 'white, any people. I think people cuss about any religions because they cuss you about your face colour. You're black. I don't like you ... Your eyes, and mouths. Some people say my eyes look really Chinese. I feel a bit angry... The way people dress up, like people wearing a sari and other people making fun of them and laughing at them. [I want to change where I live] – stop the robbings, people come at night. They try to break in – they smashed the windows with a bottle. My mum was praying downstairs and we were upstairs, someone came to try and smash our windows and me and my sister quickly put on the light, and I was lucky I didn't get the glass in my face. I was near the window.' She added an interesting aside on what she interpreted as manipulation or pressure from a teacher which exposed her to ridicule, rather than valuing her linguistic abilities. This teacher, doubtless with the best intentions, asked Farzana to read to the class in Bengali. 'I can't say no to the teacher if she asks me to read Bengali.' Why would she not want to? Farzana was silent, but her embarrassment can be understood in the context of what she had to say about the extent of racism against Bengali children.

Ethnicity, skin colour, the culture and the language of one's parents, their religious beliefs are all fundamental and inalienable parts of any person's identity. They are part of what one is born into. For a primary aged child to be asked to reject these aspects of identity or to have to face hostility about them is tantamount to rejection and denial of their fundamental source of security. Ironically, all the discourses of 'family values' recognise the centrality of family to healthy development but links are not made between racism, affiliation to family, identity and citizenship.

Issues of identity – who am I?

Race, ethnicity, religion and belonging in Britain

Children's narratives of connection and support, exclusion and violence all gave a sense of how they constructed their identities with respect to race and ethnicity. Their stories of street racism and bullying connected to colour and religion or, if they were white, their awareness and passionate rejection of racism were inextricably linked to who they felt themselves to be, in their own and in other's eyes. If you condemn behaviour you implicitly project an alternative identity – 'Not me, I'm not like that,' as white children like Rosalind and Linda made clear.

The children came in self-chosen friendship pairs and of the original twenty-three pairs I interviewed, the children in nineteen were of different ethnic backgrounds, as were fourteen of the seventeen pairs represented in this book (the exceptions were Nicholas and Alex, Jo and Derek, and Terry and John – all white English). This is heartening evidence about positive attitudes to diversity. In only two of the twenty-three transcripts was there no mention of or concern about racism and the four children concerned were all white. Some, but not all, the white children who talked about racism had relatives who were black, and were drawing on the identification and empathy rooted in strong family ties.

Testimonies of anger and pain are powerful but so too is the experience of rejection, of not being accepted as belonging here, expressed by ethnic minority children. Moreover, allegiance to their parents' original culture or country was not simple and one-dimensional. Rejected by the England they felt they belonged in, and where for the most part they had been born, they could not necessarily take comfortable refuge in an alternative identity and relationship to another country. Exhortations to 'go back where you belong' are deeply threatening if you believe you already *are* where you belong and wish to stay and be accepted, but in addition feel unsure that you would be happy and fit in where you are supposed to go. Some children were ambivalent about their heritage. Here, the issue of refugee status is particularly poignant. What can it mean to a refugee child to be told that she should go back where she belongs?

Xenophobic hostility towards refugees and immigrants is by no means new in Britain, but it can be selective, as we know from the very different experience of black and white people from the Commonwealth. As whites, neither I nor my children were ever told to 'go back where we belonged', though this was the experience of some of the black South African political refugees, who like me, could not safely return at that time. Ambivalence about ethnic and cultural identity did not feature in the discourse of every child who came from a minority community but it came through when some children felt safe enough to feel that such criticism could or would not be used against them. Many ethnic minority children were well informed by their parents about the political and economic problems in their parents' countries of origin. Children knew if their parents had been caught up and had suffered through the insecurities of West African politics, civil war or the economic problems in the Asian sub-continent or the division of Cyprus. Toyin, whose father had returned to Nigeria for a wedding, was not keen to visit her parents' country of origin. Her sister had told her she wouldn't like it. 'On the news, they're fighting and they're killing people, cos they don't like the President.' Neither Leila nor Gulsen wanted their fathers to go to Cyprus where they might get killed in 'the fighting'.

Naseem seemed alienated from the Bangladesh from which her family originated and became quite overwrought, describing nightmare-like stories of practices she did not understand (which were most certainly apocryphal). 'I'm worried about my dad going to Bangladesh', she said. 'They can take people away, they take blood and sell it. You get thrown in the street if you're still alive. They chop you up if you're not alive. A ghost caught my cousin in Bangladesh. People don't believe me, but it's true. He started getting angry and his wife died and he kept going angry. I'm worried about Bangladesh. Ghosts, people are so strange, they party at night... so strange.' Like Naseem, Farzana also believed there were dangerous ghosts 'with bulging eyes' in Bangladesh. She did not want to go there, and didn't want her family to go back either, even though her mum needed to return to visit her own mother.

Racism, aggression and belonging – who is English?

Racism is not simply a matter of white majority children ranged against black and brown minority children. When they talked about racist behaviour the children were often reluctant to reveal who the protagonists were and it required some probing to discover that abusive racist behaviour did not emanate only from white children. A few of the older children were aware of the irony of black children being abusive to other children of colour but, for the majority, abuse on the basis of colour, difference or religion was a fact of life.

The insults to Naseem described in Chapter 2 were exacerbated by racist abuse. She told me 'You get called Paki, nigger, you black shit, do you come from dog shit... Even a four year old girl... My family gets attacked. My mum especially, that's why she stays in the house all the time. It's so sad. If she goes out, my big brother and sister goes with her.'

Rosalind explained, 'They make fun of black people – 'whoever's the last one is a Paki... white children, but not me... All people with attitudes are racist. They pretend to be the boss, want to join gangs, pretend to be rude to teachers and beat people up.'

Naseem continued, 'Some people don't like people who've got different colours. They say, you come into our country, so you've got to act like us, you have to do what we tell you, this is our country and not your country.'

Rosalind thought this was ludicrous. 'People who do that are divis,' she proclaimed. 'They're stupid, they don't have to do what people tell them, just because they come from across the world doesn't mean they are any different from other people.'

Naseem's experience from four years before was still vivid: 'Yes, because when I come to this school [in Year 1], they say oh-my-god, she's mad, she's dumb, she don't know no English. She probably doesn't even have a brain, she probably doesn't even know how to fight.'

Abdul also had a story of racist abuse. 'Boys start cussing me. I was sad. They were bigger than me, around 15. If they were my age I'd have fought. Sometimes they say rude things. They were cussing my mum and about my culture. They call me Paki, and say I must go back home.'

It turns out that the boys responsible were African-Caribbean. Edward (of Nigerian heritage) had a view about this: 'They hate the people, the Jamaican boys. They're the ones that cause the trouble. They're racist.' I asked why people who are black cuss someone else who is black. Edward replied, 'They come from different places. They say, get out, you black African. I want to beat them up but there's too many and they're older.'

Toyin, (Nigerian heritage) said '... loads of people round where I live, mostly Jamaicans... if you're going to the park, if they don't like you, they say do you want to fight. This girl said she didn't like my sister and do you want to fight... We're always fighting.'

Cherise had a story about hostility between African origin and Caribbean origin people and the ways in which inflammatory situations could escalate into racist abuse when people of different ethnicities were involved. 'We've got a couple of African people in our block, we get on with them, but it can be African people against African-Caribbean. My mum nearly had a fight with an African man, because he threatened to mash up my dad's car.' 'Was that racist?' I asked, 'or just a problem about the car?' 'No,' she answered, 'he called some racist names and he said some stuff about my mum and dad. And I got a bit furious and I said how dare you say that about my mum and dad, and he got in his car and drove off and my dad got pretty angry.'

For Francesca, a light-skinned girl who had Irish, Scottish, black Zimbabwean and Jamaican in her family tree, racism could come at her from both directions, and identity could be complicated. 'Lots of white people are nice to you,' she said. 'I can't just say it's white people. It's both.' She was aware that being of mixed parentage did not guarantee acceptance in either camp in some parts of the world. She told me in some detail about her grandfather, a Zimbabwean who she said 'looks white' but was not, who had been asked to get off a black bus when he lived in Zimbabwe and who had been in danger of getting shot if he went into either a black people's club or a white people's club. 'You even get shot if you go in the wrong club,' she mused.

Francesca used a thought-provoking expression: 'I haven't been *accused* yet about my colour, but I did hear that it does happen' (my italics). Like many children, she was wary of public playgrounds because they were potential sites of racist behaviour. 'There's a little playground,' she told me. 'Every single time I go down there my mum says watch out for racist people because they can bully you.'

Cherise agreed that playgrounds were danger zones and wanted to make a clear distinction between people who were 'mental' and thus not fully responsible for their actions, and racists, who should be held responsible. 'There's a playground at the back of our block... but the Seacole goes there (a gang that called itself after the name of the estate). They destroy everything. There's a big percentage of racist people on the Seacole. They have a problem there, it's not just like they are mental people, they're racist.'

Ibrahim said, 'I always tell my brother or my father if bullies go for me. Once I went for a bully even though he was bigger. I punched him and run. I asked him why he was doing it. The bully said because he hated Pakis. He was Christian, he was brown.' Simon picked up this theme, 'Black children are cussing other mixed-race children and quarter caste, black people are accusing whites. The neighbours were throwing stuff out their windows into our garden. They kept being racist to us, saying they'll get their cat on to us (sic). They're exactly the same colour as us, using racist swearwords.'

Ibrahim said feelingly, 'I don't like racist people. I wish I could do something. They don't know how it feels. They think it's fun. One day they'll see what it's like for someone to cuss them. It's really upsetting. They call you Paki. Say you're different, you don't belong here... Elias (a Caribbean boy) acts like he's got no idea about racism. He calls Tony a white —— and Tony cusses back.'

Assia, who was Moroccan, told me that 'half caste children' called her names when she came back from karate... 'They use the B word and the F word.'

Leila (Turkish-Cypriot) and Chrissy (white) also spoke of children using the currency of racism against each other but gave disturbing details of real dislike and abuse. 'I think we were racist,' Leila said, 'because if you're just having a fight, then you just say that, because that's the only thing you can say to black people... because you can hardly say anything else.' I asked, 'So you don't really dislike black people? Do you think you're just using their colour as a way of hurting them?' Leila and Chrissy talked almost in unison. 'Yeh,' Leila replied. 'But some people, there is, there is some people... they just don't like them. I mean their colour. Because they think that they're all...' Chrissy butted in, 'Yeah they hate them because they...' and Leila completed the sentence, '... really dance and stuff, when they dance, they like, you know the way they dance, people just don't like the way they dance, and they think they're all disgusting and horrible and they think... yeah... chocolate bars.'

Where do Leila and Chrissy identify themselves in this unpleasant scenario? They are the same girls who talked earlier about pain and guilt when children are abused, how they cared and felt sorry for people who were being picked on, and how they made a point of trying to comfort them. On the other hand, Leila had already owned up to using racist abuse, and this is a worrying example of how easy it can be to fall back on racist stereotypes and slip into racist language 'because that's the only thing you can say to black people'. However, Leila's own insight and the girls' joint sense of injustice have a pay-off, as the next part of the transcript revealed.

Chrissy seemed able to use her insight and understanding in another context where she might have slid into racist stereotyping herself. She told a long story about being abused in a shop by a girl she didn't know, who 'hissed her teeth at me, and then she went 'do you want a slap round the face?', and then ran off when Chrissy went to her mum for help. Trying to work out how this story connected with what we had just been discussing, I asked, 'Was she a black girl?' 'Yeah,' Chrissy replied. Interested about whether Chrissy inevitably defined antagonism between people of different ethnicities as racism, I asked, 'So was she being racist to you, do you think?' Her answer made it clear that in Chrissy's view 'jealousy' and not racism lay behind the girl's threatening behaviour: 'She wasn't being racist.

She was just being horrible. It was spite with her, because one of them goes, you buy £60 kickers, £60 kickers...' Leila concurred, 'She was jealous of her... yea jealous.'

Threats and name-calling were part of the normal fault lines in relationships, including in school, and not always interpreted by the children as reflecting racial antagonism. However, violence and racism were regularly linked, both descriptively and as explanations, and children understood that racism underpinned the violence and bullying that haunted the lives of people of colour.

In a dialogue in which the phenomenon of finishing each other's sentences and thinking jointly is evident, Linda (white) and Shakira (African-Caribbean) described the racist name-calling on their estate. This was almost invariably accompanied by violence of one sort or another:

> Linda: Swearing...
>
> Shakira: when, when they swear, when they punch, when they kick...
>
> Linda: when they throws bottles at you ...
>
> Shakira: and they say like stuff ...
>
> Linda: about your colour... Well they say this ... this colour and they could say like something that you're a...
>
> Shakira: and like sometimes like they say, like mars bar and stuff ...
>
> Linda: yeh
>
> Shakira: and like they say it to white people as well, and like they say milky bar and stuff, but that's all ...
>
> Linda: they're being racist.

The theme of racism threaded through the interview with Stephen and Billy. As with Shakira and Linda, you can discern how each boy's line of reasoning followed closely on what his friend offered. They were describing a notorious incident when a supply teacher, Miss S, had used physical restraint to try and control the class. 'She was dragging people, and slinging them on the floor, and she hurt Michael, he was the strongest in the class, she banged his head right on the table' they explained between them. Stephen added, 'and Jimmy started being cruel to her and she was chasing him, he was calling her a monkey.' Billy interrupted, 'I think that might have been racism, remember she is black, and monkeys are brown, aren't they.'

The boys revived the discussion of racism later in the interview when I asked under what conditions they would fight for their country. They seemed to be trying to sort out what constitutes racism and trying to explain Stephen's former racist behaviour. Stephen said he would fight 'when it's racism, black on white, sorry, white on black'. Billy disagreed with him. 'Not all the time,' he said, 'Michael is always on white people ... and he's black.' Stephen however, wanted to distinguish between individual and national actions, 'Yeah, but I'm talking about countries,' he countered. He had a confession to make. 'I used to be a bit racist, cos I said uh black people are disgusting, but now I'm not racist, because that was when I was five.' 'And he didn't understand which is good or bad,' Billy offered in mitigation.

Stephen said that racism made him angry; Billy pointed out the ironies of some children's racist behaviour but also provided an insight into his own perspective: 'like Jimmy did to Miss S, but his own cousin's black, he's being racist to himself. My cousin is black. I've got a girl cousin and a boy.' 'Do they sometimes say people are racist to them?' I asked. 'Yeah, they say they're really sad, and they... instead they don't want to get in trouble, but they... so they just tell the law... and the council.' I had a surprise coming. 'What I was trying to get at, Stephen,' I said, 'is that Billy has explained to me that one of the reasons he cares about racism, is he's got two cousins who are black, so he's got some reason, because he's closely connected.' 'Yeah, and my grandpa's black,' Stephen informed me ... 'but even if there was nobody in the family that you care about ... I still think it's bad.'

It is clear from these transcripts that 'celebratory multiculturalism', which does not take on the nature of racism, is misleading and patronising about identity and misses opportunities for effective work on citizenship. Communities are not understood merely in terms of festivals and lifestyles, and the identity of their children is not adequately represented through approaches of this kind.

Identity and religion

Religion was a powerful part of some children's identity. When I asked Toyin and Farzana (Y4) what the most important thing in life was, Toyin said 'I only really like God. Other people should know about God. It says in the commandments, Jesus son of God. Some people don't believe, I try and tell my friends, they don't really believe.' Mohamed and Angus (Y3) introduced religion several times in their interview. Like Toyin, Mohamed's religion was the most important thing in his life. He would like to change 'all the Muslims, I know they care about their religion, I would like to change them ... I want them to believe in Islam, I want to teach them.' ' I like it,' he said, 'and I like to be a Muslim. I can't explain how it's nice. My family second, religion first.' Angus put religion third, after life itself and his family. 'My whole family is Christian,' he explained. I don't know if I go to church, I've just started being a Christian, it's nice anyway.' Mohamed concluded that what differentiated Christians and Muslims was that 'Christians might say life is a bit more important than religion'. Given the strength of their religious feeling, I wondered if their families approved of their friendship. Mohamed said, 'yes they do mind a bit,' then revised it to, 'no they don't mind.' Angus said, 'Christians could be brothers and sisters.'

The boys knew that religion could be the reason for conflict. Angus said, 'and they do wars because sometimes they say there are two Gods, like our God and your God.' Mohamed quickly intervened, 'Allah, there's only one God.' Angus replied, 'There's only one God yeah, but if they *say* there's two Gods, and they start fighting about it, the one lot say *our* God is better, and they say no, *our* God is better, all the people gather in from the countries...' But Mohamed was adamant, 'it doesn't matter how many gods [they say] there are, because there's only one God. They should change their mind. They shouldn't argue and be jealous. There's only one God. They should let the person believe what they want, it doesn't matter.'

Ibrahim and Simon also talked about religious wars and particularly about the Muslim-Christian conflict in Bosnia, which was in the news at the time. They were concerned that I should know that even if they found themselves in a situation of civil war they would not turn on each other, even though they came from different religious backgrounds. The title of this book is taken from Ibrahim's thoughtful response: 'It doesn't matter what religion you are, you're still a human being, we should all help each other, because you're still a human, you're not an alien from outer space.'

Most of the children of South Asian heritage talked about 'being cussed' for their religion, indicating the serious consequences to good relationships of sectarianism. Ironically, as the passages above show, Muslim children were much more likely than others to be explicit about tolerance of other religions.

Ayshe felt that children were 'horrible' to one another because of their religion, and that the school was tokenistic in its response to Muslim children. 'In our assemblies there are two teachers who usually do them, they usually just talk about Christians. They don't usually talk about Muslims and Catholics and other religions. They talked about Muslims last month [beginning of Ramadan], but that's about the only time, they talk about other religions when it's like Christmas for them.... They should talk about all religions, so that every day you don't have to hear about just Christians. I'm not saying I don't like hearing abut it, except it's not fair for other religions that they have to hear about just what the teachers want to talk about.'

Rabbi Julia Neuberger argues that the requirement that religious education in state schools be 'broadly Christian' is 'saying that those who cannot describe any part of their identity as broadly Christian do not fit' (Neuberger, 1995:233). As long as a person's religious affiliation is an important part of their identity, we need a multi-faith approach which genuinely regards all faiths as equal, with no one religion patronising or assuming superiority over another. This means putting into practice Attainment Target Two of the guidelines for religious education, currently honoured more in rhetoric than practice in many primary schools, to teach tolerance and understanding through religion rather than merely teaching about specific religious observances.

What shall we do – identity, racism, religious intolerance and citizenship

Racism and democracy are totally incompatible and national identity is deeply compromised for some people by the experience of racism, regularly associated with religious abuse. This chapter has given a glimpse of the reality of racism experienced by children in our schools, and has indicated that even children who are not personally abused are fully aware of racism, and affected by it. The arguments for tackling and challenging racism within the school and making it a no-go zone for racism need no reiteration here and indeed, no child suggested that racism was tolerated within either school. However this is by no means sufficient. When I asked Naseem what her family thought they should do about the abuse they had suffered, she shrugged and said, 'Tell the headteacher. But they pretend they're going to do something, but they don't.' 'Do teachers talk about this?' I asked. There was no reply.

Despite the Macpherson Inquiry's admonitions (1999), the education system offers no strategies to confront the violence and abuse of racism or to help children understand its roots in the histories of colonialism and exploitation. Schools appear to attribute racism to lack of understanding of other cultures. That children sometimes used the language of cultural difference as their weaponry (wearing saris, being smelly) would seem to justify positive multicultural counter-approaches, but it has never been clear to me why learning about festivals or enjoying a curry might cure the intolerance, abuse and victimisation that the children reported. Though stereotypes and ignorance contribute to racism, racist people are not convinced of the inhumanity of their ways by sympathetic introductions to 'ethnic' music or 'other' religious practices. Racism requires a political and historical analysis which considers how power for some is protected and maintained, how some white people deny that ethnic minority people are full citizens and how some ways of doing things are set up as norms against which other people are judged. The way in which some minority children appropriated the language of white racism to attack other minority children is worrying, confirming the diversity of experience and culture among the different ethnic groups and revealing underlying issues about power.

Why should children not be susceptible to rational arguments and explanations which ask them to consider common humanity, justice and rights? Learning a little about festivals is no substitute. The transcripts show that some children do condemn antisocial racist behaviour and draw on ideas about compassion, justice and tolerance. The children, white and black, who talked about coming to each others' aid, about caring for each other, who understood the irony of black/minority children abusing other people of colour – who used the language of solidarity – were a long way along the road of tackling racism. For teachers, understanding the thinking of *un*prejudiced children, who are strongly *in favour* of equality and democracy, can provide strategies to work with prejudiced and undemocratically minded individuals. If you are 'not an alien', you belong. You share a common humanity, rights and responsibilities.

I have no space to give examples from another set of interviews with the same children, which I conducted separately, but I have evidence that some of the children who spoke out against racism drew on historical knowledge about situations in which institutional racism was at the heart of victimisation. For example, Simon talked about the tragedy of children being set against each other for religious reasons during pogroms; Toyin knew that religion and ethnicity lay beneath political conflict in Nigeria; Cherise's heroes were Martin Luther King and Nelson Mandela; and Jackie and Mena both said they would not be prepared to defend a system in which white and black people were separated, like South Africa before the democratic changes of 1992. All these children responded with passion to opportunities to discuss resistance to racism.

What are the implications of the material in this chapter for the citizenship curriculum? The first is that teachers should be ready and able to discuss the events in children's lives that occur outside the school. Naseem was not the only one who thought parents should be able to come to the school for help. Some headteachers do know what is happening in their communities, having built up trusting relationships with parents who come in and seek advice and support. After this research was finished, the head of Sylvia Pankhurst school became involved with improvements to the Pankhurst estate funded through the Single Regeneration Fund, which included improving safety from racist attacks. This is an example of outreach which makes contact with community groups who are themselves trying to tackle racism, and which provides opportunities to deal with children's cynicism about where they will get help and involve them in potential solutions (though this may not be what the writers of the Guidance meant about community involvement).

Secondly, reducing racism to a matter of personal failings backfires: that is what the children will reproduce, leaving them little space for more powerful understandings and, later in their lives, for making interventions. Though it can be hard to move discussion on, racism is not just about individual people being nasty to one another, and children need to be helped to see the bigger picture. When the only explanations for difference are personalised and depoliticised, and the only strategies for understanding the real experience of minority groups are multiculturalism and celebration of diversity, children themselves are as likely as not to use 'my culture' and 'their culture' as barriers, and still to be left without the means to understand and deal with racism. This does not mean there is no point or value in multicultural work, but that it is not enough on its own. One needs to recognise and build on the antiracist and human rights concerns that many children already express. The commonly expressed view that 'people can believe what they like' cannot match a human rights approach which emphasises common-core, ethical principles which unite rather than divide, and respect for everyone's humanity, captured by Ibrahim in his phrase 'you're human, you're not an alien from outer space'.

In the light of the children's own experience outside school, it appears that in the curriculum we pussyfoot around difficult issues which are clearly within children's understanding and emotional tolerance. Literature and history both present opportunities to learn about the experience of racism and about resistance to it. Cherise could hardly be restrained from telling me the whole story of

Journey to Jo'burg (Naidoo, 1985). Farzana and Toyin had been deeply affected by learning from their teacher in Y3 the previous year about the treatment of Australian Aboriginal children taken away from their families and brought up as white. Simon, Ibrahim and Nicholas all told me about grandfathers who had fought in World War Two and knew from home, not from school, that Nazism involved killing people because of their religion and ethnicity.

Such work gives children a chance to talk about their own feelings and knowledge, and places religious intolerance and racism in its wider context as the transgression of human rights.

4

Staying safe: drugs, sex, family problems

> *I think we don't always understand words adults say. Like really hard words. We'd understand if the person said it right... we'd understand...* Farzana (aged 9)

Keeping safe – children's fears of violent crime

Shortly before I conducted the research used in this book, two particularly horrific events took place. They happened many miles from the homes and schools of any of the children but it was clear that they had made a great impact on them. First, a toddler, Jamie Bulger, was enticed away from a shopping centre by two ten year olds and brutally murdered. Secondly, a man went on the rampage with a shotgun in an infants' school in Dunblane, and a number of children were killed. In 2000 two children were horribly murdered – Sarah Payne in Surrey and Damilola Taylor in Peckham. Tabloids and television devoted considerable space to these events, and once again a sense of moral panic, anxiety and fear was transmitted by the national media, absorbed by children as well as their parents.

Children's feelings of vulnerability to mindless violence are apparent in many of the transcripts. In a shop in Nunhead, a mile or two south of where Damilola was killed, my (adult) daughter talked to a ten year old who had a large stick poking out of his coat. At first he didn't want to tell her what it was for, but after a bit he owned up. He was terrified that he might be attacked as Damilola had been, even though he lived some way away and did not go to the same school. He had taken the advice of his granny to arm himself for his own protection.

My daughter asked whether he had talked to anyone at school about his fears. The answer was no. Although the school had acknowledged Damilola's tragic death in an assembly, the teachers apparently did not realise how severely the local children were traumatised.

Earlier in the year in which I was interviewing children, a sixteen year old boy was attacked and murdered on the Seacole estate by other teenagers. This made the local papers, but not the national press. Except for the middle-class children living some distance away, virtually every child from Mary Seacole school referred to this killing, including those who did not live on the estate itself. It was another indication of how the experience of working and middle-class children differs. Working-class children are not insulated from information about their own communities and know about any violent crime. And such events happen frequently enough to fuel anxiety.

In the transcripts children regularly referred to the dangers from a variety of sources that threatened their safety. Local reality and the tragedies which were widely publicised in the press were the source of their and their families' fears and vigilance. Children, including some boys who otherwise presented themselves as tough and rather macho, feared being snatched, taken away and killed. Others were afraid of being mugged. For some, child abuse from 'strangers' was the issue. Terry's mother had told him about two little girls who were wandering around alone outside the school, and now Terry was worried about his brother in the infants – 'any kind of man could have got out and took them... so there should be security and cameras and all that in the school so people couldn't just run out.' Later in the interview Terry returned to this theme – 'I'd like to change all these strangers, you can't even go to play out in the streets because of these.'

Fear of strangers interfered with Billy's football. 'Well,' he said, 'it's fun going football training and everything on the grass, but when we've got tournaments we got to go down the grass on our own and wait for Chris our manager, and sometimes we've got to sit around and wait, and we can get taken away and killed.' 'Who by?' I asked. Billy replied, 'cos round the Seacole there's loads of people ...there's been people killed round the Seacole and there's no one down on the grass with us, there's only us little kids, eight, nine year olds, and we can just get taken away and killed.'

'At nine thirty in the morning, do you think that might happen to you?' I pressed.

'Yeah,' he replied. His friend Stephen was fed up that his mum wouldn't let him play out but he understood her reasons. 'She says as soon as it gets dark you've got to come in and it gets dark at four o'clock and I've got to come straight in. She says I'm not letting you come in at that time [half past seven]. I might get stolen, I might be taken away.' Billy picked up on this and said he was worried about getting beaten up, and worried about 'getting stolen, if my mum lets me go out until half seven when it gets dark.'

Eight year old Angus from the Pankhurst Estate was afraid lest strangers be mentally ill and dangerous – 'I don't like it if someone's not normal, a bit sick in the mind, like they're going to kill someone.'

Sex, prostitution, teenage pregnancy

Sex was an infrequent subject for discussion but a few children indicated that they had personal knowledge about sex and that it was a source of concern. Is this is the tip of an iceberg or is it very unusual? My hope is that you will find the material that follows helpful in opening up a world of childhood of which you may not be fully aware, since schools do not make space for children to talk about their lives in the way I was able to as a researcher.

Edward and Abdul (Y5) introduced sex into the interview quite early on. Abdul was giggling uncontrollably about a private joke, and Edward said 'Abdul always laughs when he sees someone naked. There was a man and a woman behind the dustbins...' and then he cracked up too and was unable to continue. Later, when they were invited to put their own questions, Abdul asked ' why do people have sex?' I gave the standard explanation that this was the way babies are made, and if we didn't have new babies, there'd soon be no people, that you needed to be old enough, and both people needed to enjoy it, not just one person. Abdul listened, then observed. 'Some people try it out but if they don't get a boy they move out and get another woman.' 'That's why they use condoms, so they can't get babies,' Edward noted, and then he took me by surprise. 'I know a boy,' he said, ' he was jumping on his sister.'

Cherise and Francesca also introduced sex into the discussion. Francesca's reply to what made her sad about how other people behaved was hard to follow at first and seemed incoherent. But gradually what she was saying fell into place. She was talking about prostitutes, and I suspected that her incoherence was because of her difficulty in speaking about such a painful subject. I had started to notice that using the third person was a common device used by the children to distance themselves from the people in a story, whereas in reality, the characters might be close to home, or they themselves.

'I suppose when they do *it* to you .. 'it'... I mean it's just very sad, and sometimes it does make you like angry... and it isn't just because it's people picking them up and all that .. if this person like is a bad person and like if they're gonna get... I mean.. they give 'em some... if somebody's really really bad and after that, say they murder them.' 'Yeh,' Cherise agreed in solidarity and Francesca went on with more confidence. 'I know, because they're not sure what's going to happen to them. I mean just going past, just earning money... and I think the reason why they do this is because they've got problems, and it's mostly grown-ups... I mean it's either they've got bills to pay and they can't find a job and after that they just think I have to just do this for my children, you know, say like if they've got children... Yeah, and the reason why young teenagers do it is I mean is because they've either had, I mean they've got problems of their own, it's either about school, I mean if they get bullied a lot at school, because I know this girl, I mean my cousin knows her, and, and I know she started doing it because she had troubles with her mum, arguing and, it's also because about her dad, it's just like problems like that and she also gets bullied at school, so... they just can't take the pressure and they just do stupid things to make it go away.'

Francesca's theorising about the underlying causes of teenage prostitution becomes still more poignant in the light of other matters she talked about, specifically that her parents did not get on and that she felt deeply insecure about whether they might split up, which would have knock-on effects on the financial stability in her family. Francesca did not say that she was bullied at school, but I found myself wondering how far this story about teenage prostitution reflected genuine anxiety that she might be pushed into this way of life because of the insecurities in her home life.

Cherise said that in addition to teenage prostitution ('like Francesca says') she was concerned about teenage mothers. Unlike Francesca's careful maintenance of anonymity in her story about prostitution, Cherise made it clear that she was talking about members of her own family, and that she disapproved of irresponsible attitudes to having babies. 'Some people in my family have their children when they are fifteen or something... When you're a teenage mother you are pregnant with a child. You decide to have an abortion because you knew you was going to have the child. And when you have the child then you complain about it. It's not nice. When I have a child I have to become responsible for me and my child, and I can't keep playing, or school ... it isn't because of my age, it's because of what I've done to myself, to make me bigger. When you're a teenage mother you wish that you never had your child at that age, because you say, look at all the things I've missed out on, can't go out to parties and everything, and that's what teenage mothers, I don't really like them for, because there's nothing wrong with them, it's just when they complain about not going out, when they knew they was going to get themselves into a muddle. That's what I don't like.'

Francesca followed with a story about teenage pregnancy in her family and the trouble this caused. 'My grandma's sister, she's got a daughter and she got pregnant at seventeen years old. And then it's just, there was like problems, because my grandma's sister, she was saying, oh how am I going to look after their child, and she has to take her, I mean she has to look after her own child for herself, and I'm not going to look after it for her, I mean it's her fault that she got pregnant.'

Cherise developed the theme of responsibility for one's own actions, taking both her own voice and that of her mother. 'What happens, what happens mostly with teenage mothers, is when you dump your child off with your mum, and your mum's a grown woman, she's done the looking after, she had looking after you, and if you have any brothers or sisters she's done the looking after them, why should she look after your child? It does sound mean, but it isn't mean, because your mother has a life of her own.' Now she took the voice of the mother, 'You have a life of your own, and you've got a child that needs a life of her own, and you can't keep on dumping your child off on me.' Then she reverted to her own voice: 'In some ways it is important to go and get a job now. That's fine [to have a baby] if you're doing nothing, but I'd never like to have a child and do that because my mother would love to have a grandchild, but she wouldn't like it every minute. Because you don't dump your baby off, and be that kind of mother.'

Sex and strangers

Sexual abuse is hinted at in the way child abuse is tackled in schools, generally through specially written material. Such material still portrays 'strangers' as the perpetrators of unwanted 'touching', whereas all the evidence indicates that people who are close to or even part of the child's own family are far more likely to be implicated. Danger from strangers was the stereotype the children offered. This hardly seems helpful, particularly because, as the transcripts show, their notions of 'strangers' were linked to mental derangement, drug abuse and generally recognisably peculiar behaviour, far removed from the ordinary, unremarkable, familiar people who might be potential abusers.

Several children introduced the dangers that lay in wait from sexual predators, and discussed the difficulties of distinguishing between genuine friendship offered in good faith by older people and exploitation. Drawing on books that had been read to them at school, personal knowledge from home, television and parental advice, all the children used the prevalent and erroneous stereotype of 'strangers' as the perpetrators of child abuse. It was particularly notable that the concept of 'stranger' had itself become distorted. It is difficult in light of the way the children talked about 'strangers', to imagine the story of the Good Samaritan impressing them as a role model. Children in the inner city estates had been taught by their families to treat strangers with the utmost caution and suspicion and to take the possibility of child abuse very seriously.

Seven year old Gulsen explained when it was acceptable to 'face (i.e.deal with) people if they are being nasty to you'. 'If it's really really horrible,' she said, 'not like school things, but if someone tries to touch you anywhere, then you'd have to do that [smack them round the face]. I mean like strangers, like someone you don't know, and if someone touches you.' Talking across Akosua who was trying to get a word in, she implied personal knowledge about child abuse and explained the importance of leaving a mark on someone who attacked you. 'Well my friend ... there was a grown-up ... in court they might say I was lying that he touched me. If somebody does touch you, you must prove it. You *must* hurt them, because otherwise you're going to die, and you don't want yourself to die.' Gulsen reckoned that it was extremely important to know about child abuse and to know what to do ... 'you have, you have to do something, I've heard it, my mum's talked, I've talked about it to my mum. I think I should know about it ... because like, imagine if something did happen to you, and you wouldn't know what to do...' The main thing in her view was to be extremely watchful and suspicious of strangers. 'You just watch another person ... then you have to see what they're gonna do, and then if you're gonna take (cos you watched the person) like a drug, like they're gonna say would you like a sweetie, but it can be a drug and you say no.'

Linda and Shakira (Y5) had similar views about the possibility of strangers enticing them with sweets. They were talking about how dangerous life could be on the estate... 'People have been killed about guns and stuff ... knives,' Shakira said. Linda's story reiterated the dangers of strangers: 'When me and my best friend, and we like went to a party and ... sometimes we see people that we're really not sure about, and so like we move out of the way, but we're always concerned because like they might have something in their pocket ... and everyone knows this, that if they're a stranger and they ask what the time is, you don't go to their car...and if they say do you want this sweetie and stuff, you stay away.' A little while later Shakira returned to this theme, 'Yeah, because some people think that it's just men, but it's ladies too. And some people say better watch out for that man and like they think it's only men strangers who...' She tailed off, unwilling or unable to elaborate further.

It turned out that for some children, the very word 'stranger' carried disturbing baggage and connotations. A stranger was seldom acquainted with one's family (though they might be) but was peculiar, abnormal and untrustworthy. Strangers got the better of children by enticing them with cakes and sweets which were drugged. 'I've heard a true story...' Gulsen told me, 'Well, there's this man who lives across the road, a bit like nutty... and he came on my brother's birthday, he bringed round a birthday cake ... and like if you're a bit strange, I don't think you should eat it, they might have put drugs in it or something.' Later Gulsen wanted to discuss the question: 'would you like somebody that's a stranger to be your friend?' Akosua answered, 'I don't think so, because they might, might harm you ... what I think is no, they shouldn't, because they might touch you everywhere and...' She tailed off and I asked whether it was possible for strangers to be nice people, or not. Akosua replied, 'It isn't possible, I don't think strangers will be nice friends to other people ... not like school friends ... they are strangers like ... like they're not in your family, someone isn't in your family, that means they're strangers to you.' Gulsen thought you shouldn't mix with poor people, 'because they might be a bit strange, because they live on the street, and no one like, really tells them anything ... because sometimes they do look quite horrible.'

Good Samaritans?

Neither Mena nor Jackie (Y6) would walk around on the estate at ten o'clock at night though it was not completely clear how far they separated anxiety about being mugged from potential sexual violence. 'It's not safe, it's not a safe place. I don't think it's a safe place', Jackie said emphatically.' Mena said, 'if you walk past they just look at you'. 'Does that make you feel uncomfortable?' I asked. 'Mmh,' Mena said, 'I'm scared to go down there. I run if I see boys.' But these were not strangers. Both Mena and Jackie said they knew these people. Jackie said, 'My uncle used to hang around with them, but he doesn't hang around with them no more. That's how I know most of them.'

To become involved with strangers held another kind of danger, according to Jackie and Mena. They had talked about mugging on the Pankhurst state, and how they had watched out of the window as an old man was attacked. Probing their sense of community responsibility, I asked if they thought everybody should be allowed to behave just as they pleased on the estates. 'If they're not doing anything to my family, I would,' Jackie said. Mena said she would stick up for their class-mate Fauzia (she of the tin can story in Chapter 2). 'But strangers, no?' I asked, thinking of the old man they had just talked about. Jackie was frankly incredulous. 'Strangers?' she echoed, in a voice that implied that I'd asked her to come to the aid of a rearing cobra. 'Yes,' I tried to explain, ' if you saw someone attacking someone who was a stranger.' Jackie's reply put her incredulity at my question into context. Strangers were not simply people one did not know, but people who were inherently and by definition dangerous. 'I might care,' she said, 'but sometimes I don't really like going up to other people ... if the person is still there.' 'I wouldn't,' Mena said, in a voice which brooked no debate. I persisted, 'Do you think their behaviour should be stopped, even if not by you, that's what I'm asking, or is it really their own business?' 'Yeh, yeh, stopped by other people, but if like they're fighting and like one person's winning, the other one's badly hurt and the person's still there [the attacker] I wouldn't go up to them, cos sometimes I could get into something quite serious.'

The first time you might become actively aware of children's fears could be on a school journey, when it becomes apparent that far from being a peaceful haven, the countryside is perceived as harbouring all manner of potential monsters, ready to jump out from every hedgerow. The extent and depth of children's anxieties should give us pause. Is it enough to give advice about not talking with strangers, not going out alone? What about the consequences for their mental health of their knowledge about violence against children, even if it is exceptional, rare and far away? Shouldn't children have the opportunity to talk about their fears and their horror at what they know can happen? Shouldn't we help them sort out the confusions that arise because adults are not straight and honest with them?

In view of children's anxieties and the probable reality, how one approaches mutual social responsibility in a community becomes problematic, even as an issue for discussion. If children know that an attacker might carry a knife or a gun, it is simply stupid to intervene, however much they empathise with the victim. As Jackie pointed out, one 'could get into something quite serious.' Even if one acknowledges that children are not in a position to intervene against people who are bigger, stronger and more powerful, how does one get them to consider situations where they might at least be physically equal and what they might do when they are older? Jackie and Mena thought they knew what was needed on the estate – better lighting and better policing. A programme funded by the EC and the Single Regeneration Fund came up with exactly those solutions for the Pankhurst Estate. Solutions for the Seacole Estate were even more dramatic, and have resulted in the demolition of whole areas of internal walkways, rebuilding, doing away with the secluded places where gangs could gather, installing sealed security entrances and rethinking the planning of all the entries, exits and public spaces.

Point 2a in the Key Stage 2 guidance suggests that children should 'research, discuss and debate topical issues, problems and events'. Taking a responsible attitude as a citizen entails learning about pressure groups and considering community-based solutions, thus going beyond teaching children how to protect themselves personally. Such work is well within the scope of the geography or design technology curriculum. It need not be marginalised through a subject which is non-statutory and addressed largely through circle time.

Homophobia and homosexuality

Homophobia as a form of victimisation and abuse is not faced openly in the PSHE guidance. This, I believe, has its roots in official ambivalence about homosexual partnerships, which even though legal, are still considered by many people as inferior to heterosexual relationships and by some as shameful, wicked and against religious principles. The long shadow of anxiety and intolerance about homosexuality, enshrined in Section 28, hangs over the world of education, more than twelve years after the bill was originally put through parliament. In 2000, New Labour tried and failed to get this item removed from the Statute book.

Two things are needed before homophobia and homophobic stereotyping can be tackled: the first is to acknowledge the extent of homophobic behaviour between children. The second is for teachers to have the courage of their convictions that homophobia is discriminatory, hurtful and antisocial and that it is at the root of some vicious aggression on the part of intolerant adults. Since much of what occurs in KS 2 is understood to be preparing children for their future roles in society, it seems extraordinary to ignore the extent of homophobia in the primary school and not challenge it. The silence simply condones bigotry.

To take on homophobia, teachers need to interpret the wording in the guidance in a positive and proactive way. For KS 3 (where citizenship education is compulsory and not just guidance) pupils are to be taught about the effects of *all kinds* of stereotyping, prejudice, bullying, racism and discrimination and how to challenge them assertively, and to recognise the range of lifestyles and relationships within society' (my emphasis). The KS 2 guidance is far weaker. Children should be *aware of* different types of relationships, including marriage and those between friends and families; and *realise the nature and consequences* of racism, teasing, bullying and aggressive behaviours. They should ask for help against such aggression, and *recognise and challenge* stereotypes.

In the face of anxiety about homosexuality, rational discussion about homophobia as a form of discrimination, bullying and aggression can be difficult. However, that Damilola Taylor was taunted by his peers as 'gay' in the weeks before his murder in November 2000, brought largely unrecognised homophobia among young children into the limelight. To be called 'gay' or 'lezzie' in the primary school world is to be branded as abnormal and an outsider. The words are not used as neutral descriptors, such as 'tall' or 'brown haired'. But words change and gain new meanings. Just as 'cool', as in 'that's cool', or 'he's acting cool', does not have much to do with temperature, so, according to an article in the *TES* in January 2001, 'gay' has been redefined to mean stupid.

In Chapter 2 we saw how children regularly used sexually insulting words to wound and abuse, generally with reference to mothers, though sometimes about each other. Two children mentioned the use of homophobic epithets 'poof' and 'pussy' about boys. The connection of homosexuality with physical or mental impairment was implied in Jackie's remark that some boys shouted 'pussy' at her uncle who has special needs. Linda explained what it meant to insult someone's mother by saying she was a 'poof' or 'gay': even though she thought you 'couldn't really say this about a woman', it was a common way to abuse someone's mother and translated to mean stupid.

We may never know whether children were suggesting that Damilola Taylor was homosexual or that he was stupid. Genuine homophobia does, however, exist in primary schools. In a school I was involved with (not as part of this research), I was informed about a veritable 'epidemic' of homophobic behaviour, as the teachers called it, which spread like wildfire through both Y6 classes. Following a school disco, several boys were taunted as 'poofs' by other children. Notices were secretly pinned on their backs alleging they were poofs, and children indulged in all the usual stereotypical limp-wrist mockery. This went on for the best part of a week. At a loss about what to do, the teachers lectured culprits and banned such behaviour, but were aware that this was a weak response. Though the school had a strongly worded and actively implemented antiracist policy, they had no statement about equal opportunities with respect to sexism or homophobia, and were wrong-footed by the incident. It is likely that they hoped the problem would 'go away' and that they wouldn't have to think about it till the next time.

As part of their anti-bullying and equal opportunities policies, schools could discuss contemporary examples of homophobic intolerance and consider making children aware through the overt curriculum of how homophobia has affected people in the past. Many adults who know about the fate of Jews in Nazi Germany and the discriminatory practice of forcing Jews to wear a yellow star, are unaware that homosexuals were forced to wear a pink triangle, were routinely rounded up into camps and that up to 10,000 were exterminated simply because of their sexual orientation.

How many children who have read and loved Oscar Wilde's fairy tale *The Selfish Giant* know that he was imprisoned for homosexuality 100 years ago, and emerged a broken man? It is worth considering, too, that the soaps primary school children watch, such as East Enders and Brookside, increasingly take on such issues. Is it a case once again of teachers being out of synch with the world that children inhabit?

Drugs

The PSHE guidance states clearly that part of developing a healthy, safe lifestyle is knowing what affects mental health, how to make informed choices, which commonly available substances and drugs are legal and illegal, their effects and risks, and how to recognise the different risks in different situations.

However, children suggested that it was not so much personal vulnerability to substance abuse that was the issue, but knowledge about and coping with abuse by others. Several children mentioned drunkenness as an explanation for violence, or the failure to maintain a reasonable lifestyle. A drunk man had hit Toyin's older sister in the park and she was now too scared to go there. Assia told how children taunted an alcoholic who lived on the streets and came knocking at their doors asking for food. Children ran after him in the street shouting 'drunk man, drunk man'. Her mum gave him food, but Assia thought he should spend his money on clothes and food, not beer. Her friend Sean's intervention was gentle and non-judgemental: 'The kids are doing the damage, not the man', he said. 'The man needs help. He needs to get a house. I would give them all houses, all the people on the street.'

Most primary school children in England have not come into personal contact with abuse of hard drugs. However, Class A drug abuse is common on large inner city estates and primary school children growing up in such environments are much more knowledgeable than one might expect or wish. The paragraphs that follow show that from the youngest in Y3, through to the oldest in Y6, there are children with personal knowledge about drug abuse, who could tell their teachers a thing or two. One can sometimes discern their hostility or fear of the effects of drugs, though for some children, drug-taking and alcohol abuse were a fact of life among older people, and their comments and reactions were non-committal.

Mohamed and Angus (Y3) spoke about drugs early in the interview. Angus said, 'I live in a flat and on the stairs there's all like wee, and I saw drugs.' Mohamed had seen people taking drugs round where he lived. 'They were hanging round early in the morning and I saw them talking to each other and when I was at the youth club I saw a pack of drugs in a plastic bag and it looked like powder and it was drugs. My parents said 'don't touch it, it might have infection on it.' Angus capped this story, 'I was out with my friend Elizabeth and I saw two boys and a group of girls on the stairs, and when the boys went, we went into there, and we saw two smoke things and loads of drugs all over the floor.' Angus worried that 'they might put drugs in all the sweets at night, and we might die, like that girl [Leah Betts] in the news.'

Gulsen, one of the youngest children I interviewed, talked about drugs in the context of child abuse by strangers. She worried that someone might gain sexual power over her by putting drugs in a cake. Although she did not suggest she was at risk of choosing to take drugs, she was aware that some drugs can knock you out, or undermine your normal ability to fight off an assailant.

Eleven year old Jackie's story about drugs is descriptive rather than judgemental or fearful. One of her uncles had been part of the 'Pankhurst gang' and she knew most of its members. She mentioned that they were pushing stolen goods like speakers, and then said in a puzzled voice 'I don't understand what they do really. All they do is stand around smoking weed.' However, she thought this affected their attitude and their self-control. 'They smoke weed, they go high, they go mad, and once you start weed, it's like they can't stop... One day, when I was walking to the shop, I saw one of them, the boy was going, where's my weed, my weed. And he punched him in his face.' I asked if the Pankhurst gang used harder drugs as well. The reply was interesting because it suggested that in Jackie's mind using drugs might be associated with courage rather than self-abuse, or health risk. 'No, just weed. Some of them aren't brave enough even to take weed.'

Ibrahim and Simon's attitude was much less sanguine. One of the things Simon worried about was that when he grew up his wife would 'use him, go off with my best friend, take drugs, because there's a lot on the Pankhurst. Some people go crazy or die,' he said. Ibrahim agreed. 'They dive from a building, they think they can fly.'

John and Terry were talking about gangs of older boys on the Seacole, who broke down the fences, smashed glass, smoked and swore...'you burn it and then you sprinkle it, and it's like, I just don't like it...' John said. Alcohol, however, seemed to be more acceptable. Terry told a story about his dad coming home from the pub 'flopping and that drunk' but the point of the story was not his being drunk but being beaten up and having to go to hospital.

Learning to deal with emotions: concern about faulty adult relationships and bereavement

There are other issues which tend to be avoided in the primary curriculum or, if touched on at all, addressed with great caution. I turn now to these issues, again raising questions about teachers' knowledge of their children's world and the relevance of the curriculum.

The first issue is bereavement. Several children talked to me about the deaths of much-loved grandparents. Many children seemed to have come to terms with these deaths, particularly if the person had lived to a good age. But those of us who have lost a dearly-loved relative or friend know that dealing with bereavement can be a slow and very unsettling process. As adults, we know that negative emotions of guilt, anger and abandonment, which can turn against the person who has died, can accompany the pain and emptiness of loss, that are hard enough to deal with on their own. While teachers may well know about a death in the family and 'make allowances' or give sensitive support on an individual basis, it is possible that more could be done. Feelings of guilt and anger could be acknowledged and children allowed to act these out, or talk them through. Such an approach is part of social and emotional education. For one thing, the children are helped to deal with emotions which might otherwise be channelled into depression or aggressive behaviour. For another, all children would be helped to consider the emotional underpinnings of other people's behaviour, including that of their parents. Thus, dealing openly with such issues becomes part of developing children's emotional intelligence.

Eight year old Mohamed's grandfather had recently died of cancer, and Mohamed felt deeply bereaved but also guilty, as if it were somehow his fault. You'll remember that he talked with great love and admiration about his grandfather. In the interview Mohamed returned several times to his guilt, and I felt that he needed, and perhaps had not had, sufficient opportunity to discuss his bereavement. Consequently, during the interview I took a little time to talk about cancer and tried to get him to express why he felt personally guilty about his grandfather's death. The situation was familiar: just as children tend to feel they are somehow responsible for divorce in their family, Mohamed, a young boy with a strong moral sense, felt that this death would not have happened if he had behaved 'better'. He also talked about not being told exactly what was going on or what had happened, being excluded from the funeral and the process of mourning by his parents, who felt his presence was not appropriate and who did not seem to appreciate the depth of his emotional turmoil. It is interesting that after we had talked, he used the very words I had used in an effort to comfort him: that people live on in the hearts of those who loved them.

Cherise and Francesca, two of the older children in the sample, also talked about bereavement and death. They thought adults and children were alike and experienced similar feelings. Cherise, whom you may remember for her assertive self-confidence, was in a different position from Mohamed, because her mother had not excluded her from knowledge about death and had shared her own feelings with her. Cherise talked about her own sadness and her mother's depression when her great-grandmother had died. 'I had a great-granny in Jamaica and my mum was very depressed and I loved her very much and she died in '94 and my mother had to take two months off work, and it was that sad.' Cherise broke down when she started talking about her aunt's death. She had viewed her aunt in her coffin, as was customary in her community.

From a teacher's perspective the important thing in this case is surely to recognise the depth of Cherise's emotional response, not just so as to make allowances for her after the event but mainly to help her through the bereavement and allow her to express her sorrow if she chose to, rather than bottle it up, as she was doing in school. Nicholas' grandmother had died the previous year but the memory was still strong. He said 'I was upset ... I was sad giving him (sic) a last kiss, and I can still think about it now.' Nicholas also knew about depression. 'A long time ago,' he said, 'my great-grandfather was a private in World War Two, and he got very frightened... so he got very ill about it and he had to retire.'

Difficult relationships at home

One hopes the classroom will be a 'safe haven' for children who are having a traumatic time in their home lives, perhaps because of incipient family breakdown or in the aftermath of fractured relationships. However, teachers have a great many contractual responsibilities which drain away time and energy. We all know colleagues who were 'burned out' by their willingness to take on some of the pressing emotional problems their pupils brought to school. In my time as a class teacher I think I probably became too involved with the problems of families already under the aegis of social services, and with hindsight I wonder whether I did much to help in the long run. I have thought long and hard about including the material that follows. If you are deeply concerned about a child's emotional well-being, you will go through the channels of support available. But the following paragraphs may help you interact and respond to their needs at an individual level in a more insightful way.

Many children suffer anxiety and pain about anger and arguments in the home. The overt curriculum does not have space for this but it is nevertheless part of mental health and coming to terms with the nature of relationships. Children living in cramped quarters with severe economic and social stress were fully aware of the tensions in their families. Several children talked about their feelings about problems in their family and I will draw on a few.

Francesca, the girl who explained teenage prostitution as girls 'who couldn't take the pressure and did stupid things to try and make it go away', told me, 'My mom and dad have a lot of arguments and I'm thinking what's going to happen if my dad leaves and my mum finds a stepfather, will I get on with him. Will I hate my dad for doing that, or if I will hate my mum.' She described feeling very scared and not knowing what was going to happen when her mum and Granny argued. She felt she was fobbed off with insincere and misguided attempts to protect her. 'I don't know why parents have arguments,' she said, 'because they should realise their own children think, because they're crying and they say it's alright, but it's *not*, because it's *not* alright. It would make it easier if they were to tell you what the argument's about.' Parents, she conceded, don't want to make their children worried. They send them to bed to get them out of the way, but, she said, 'it hurts even more when the grown-ups say it's nothing to worry about. Because you know it is something to worry about. They don't realise that you're hearing and when you're older, you will go: why didn't you explain to me when I was small? There was this thing, one day my dad came back, and my mum started shouting, and after that I said, why are you shouting, and she said 'you know' and I didn't and I was just confused and I never found out.'

Linda and Shakira also talked about witnessing adult fights. Linda tried to explain how it felt and how she became part of the argument. 'Like mum and ... dad... if there's just one little kid like me, they argue about 'can't take her that place, can't take her that place, can't take her in the car, but maybe the dad might start shouting at the mum, and you're just like on the stairs looking down the stairs at them, just shouting at each other, and you just run into your bed and stuff, and start slamming doors, and start to cry, and they just goes, 'see what you've done', and then they both run up and down the stairs, and the mum says its OK.'

Rosalind and Naseem indicated that they were party to half-understood adult rows or conversations; they tried to make sense of them, not always successfully. They seemed to confirm Francesca's view that the ensuing confusion is worse than the truth. Grown-ups told them not to interrupt or butt in, or refused to explain what they were talking about. 'I listen, I eavesdrop,' Rosalind said without any embarrassment. She went on to say that 'people ended up on the streets because they run away from home, their mum and dad get in huge arguments, so you get scared and you run away and you can't go back.' Though Naseem believed that her parents had an excellent relationship, her attempts to make sense of adult conversations which she overheard but was not allowed to ask questions about, also had a negative outcome. 'They say, you'll find out later. They have not much secrets, but they do have some,' she said. She then told a highly coloured and dubious story about people in Bangladesh getting chopped up and their blood being sold, which suggests not just a high level of fantasy but the problems of misunderstood overheard conversation.

What should we do about this knowledge?

Responding to the controversial and sensitive issues raised in this chapter must start with putting aside judgements or preconceptions about what it is suitable for young children to know, and being prepared to accept the reality of what they really do know and worry about. I have already acknowledged that the details about a child's family life are seldom the business of a class teacher, even if the headteacher knows about them and may even be giving support to the adults. Moreover, teachers are seldom trained to deal with personal difficulties. It would be insensitive to make such personal material part of the overt curriculum, to be shared by all children.

On the other hand, there are ways to support children, quite often in the short term, helping them get through a particular bad patch. One might find time to invite a child to tell you more about what is going on in a drawing, or a story they have written. Being there to listen and comfort is often enough – many people simply want to know that someone knows what is going on, without expecting any intervention. You may want to use the opportunities of drama or get children to write questions and replies to a 'problem page' or stories in the third person (a strategy children themselves used when they talked to me), all of which can preserve anonymity but still air issues and feelings. Puppets and access to the small-world toys familiar in nurseries are another safe vehicle for children to use to express emotional pain. I well remember watching a ten year old boy whose father was a severely damaged alcoholic and whose family was going through a bitter break-up, coming into my (infants) classroom after school and playing out his anxieties and feelings with Lego people.

Carefully chosen fiction is another effective support – allowing children to identify with a character, put into words the emotions they may be suppressing, understand that they are not alone, and often providing hope of an ultimate solution. Some schools even provide for anxious, sad or depressed children through access to a specially equipped room and an appropriately trained adult (see 'The Place to Be' in the Resources section).

5

Poverty and social justice

The children's attitudes to money could be represented by a parabola, with extreme poverty at one end and extreme wealth at the other. But *both* poles were seen negatively, and only the mid-point positively. At one negative pole was homelessness, begging and the humiliating situation where your parents could only afford to clothe you from a charity shop. At the other was extreme wealth, associated with selfishness, ostentatious spending and 'showing off'. Such ostentation was responsible for the misguided 'jealousy' of those who couldn't afford the luxuries and did not have a sensible value system.

The economic basis of family life

Virtually every child indicated that they believed that the purpose of a family was to support each other and the children. By support they meant physical care as well as emotional care. In this, their theories were in line with economic historians who have analysed the role of the family and theorists of child development such as Maslow, who argues that needs such as protection and food are at the base of a pyramid of needs, making possible learning, self-esteem and 'self actualisation'.

From the youngest to the oldest, children were aware that in the adult world you had to earn and manage money, that you had to support children and that sometimes this was not easy. Though it would be disingenuous to imagine that the children did not hanker after new trainers with the fashionable brand name or long for the latest craze in computer games, they expressed strikingly *un*-materialistic views about the importance of wealth in their lives. Parents and other adults subjected to nagging after expensive consumer goods might be sceptical about how genuine these expressions of value really were. Michael Billig (1987) has written at length about the contradictions and inconsistencies in most people's discourse, and so, without denying parents' experiences, we can probably take seriously the attitudes that were expressed during the interviews. It is impossible to say whether the children were a-typical, or saying what they thought I would approve of, but time and again in the context of what was important in their lives and, specifically, how important money was, children asked only to be comfortable within their family and not to struggle to pay the bills. They believed that not only children but adults and even old people needed the protective net of a family to prevent their falling into poverty. Like the horror attached to Victorian workhouses, the children saw being taken into care as one of the worst fates that could befall a child.

Several children said that difficulties about managing money led to arguments in the family. Akosua said 'He (my father) had lots of money and he just walked off, and he saw some woman, and he said hello, and she walked on, and then they got on with each other, and they start marrying each other ... and you know what my mum's upset about this, because she hasn't got enough money and she said I wish she's dead.'

Francesca and Cherise identified the need to earn money as the defining feature of adulthood. Cherise said, 'I think yes and no [about the similarities between adults and children]... You're going to work to earn a living and we're going to school to earn an education for yourself and some proudness (sic) for your mother and father. And your mother is going to work to earn some money for you and for herself.' Francesca followed this up with, 'I do think children and parents ain't the same, because they do go to work, and they do earn money for us, and there are bills to pay, and they cook for you every single night, we have to be nice to them, they're doing all this for you ... And then when you grow up get a good job and just try and make everything right.'

Later Francesca spoke about the pressure on some women to become prostitutes in order to feed their children: 'They just go in cars just to earn money ... because they've got problems, they've got bills to pay, and they can't find a job, and they think I just have to do this for my children.' In Francesca's view 'the most important thing in life is find a good job so you can pay your bills and your electricity, and you won't have any problems ... If you've got a family, then you have to look after them, and feed them. I'd put my family first, then my job second, then money third, because you would need money to look after your family.' Cherise said, 'I would be [number] one, my mother would come two, the family would be three and the friends would come down fourth. Cos you can lose your friends before you can lose your family or your mother. I would put money down below. And job.' This was a view echoed by the middle-class children in the sample, Nicholas and Alex, Emily and Harriet, all of whom called on stories about people who were rich but unhappy and had no friends, to support their view that money was not the most important thing in life.

Mohamed was concerned with the amount of money that went out in his family to pay bills. Sometimes he had to go without, but he understood about priorities. 'We have to pay the bills too much,' he said. 'And I don't like to live in a council flat. I'd like to be living in a house. They want you to pay a lot of money and I was going to get that last year for my bike, and I had to give it all away to the council, and they're still taking it off me and my family.' Angus had commented that he disliked the graffiti with 'rude words' on the walls of the flats, but Mohamed said, 'some graffiti are important, like they're for the council, they're stopping people get money from the council.'

Ibrahim indicated how important it was to be able to feed your children as part of your adult role. 'When I grow up,' he said, 'I'll have a wife and kids to support. I'll stay with my family, invite my friends to my house... I know some people who don't hardly feed their children. The children come to my house. Their mum won't give them that much stuff, but sometimes I think it's not the mum's fault. I think it's the dad's. The dad don't hardly buy any shopping.' Simon butted in, 'and the dad's probably going gambling or something.' Ibrahim let him finish, then continued, 'I don't have the guts to say why don't you feed your children? It's the father. I can't do anything about it.'

Jackie and Mena thought that most people would agree that the family was the most important thing in their lives, except for 'vain' people, who would say 'my body's the most important thing'. Using phrases which many of the children echoed, and which sounded as though they might come straight from grown-ups themselves, Jackie said, 'Your family, they's the ones that look after you, you should have some respect for them. They put clothes on you and food in your mouth.' People who thought money was the most important thing were just 'wrong', Jackie and Mena chorused. 'Money can't buy you your family,' Jackie said. 'Exactly,' Mena agreed. 'Money's the last thing in life.' Jackie continued, 'If someone's richer I don't really care. I've got what I need. It doesn't bother me.' Mena said, 'I don't need any more money. As long as you've got food in the cupboard and clothes in the bedroom.' Terry explained eloquently why love came so high on his list of important things: 'If you had lots of money', he said, 'you can't buy love with money, but with love you can do whatever you want, you can love everything, but money... if you're a rich man and you've got all this money you won't be thinking about love.'

Emily and Harriet not only dismissed money – 'that comes last, cos it's not very important' – but seemed to associate being rich with being mean and uncaring. Emily explained 'cos you could be really rich and really horrible, cos that usually happens,' and Harriet thought 'sometimes people only care about money, they don't care about being nice to people... like if you're a business manager really. It's like someone's really poor, and then they won't give them any money.' Emily picked up this theme: 'They like see them on the street asking for money, they probably wouldn't give any, cos they were so horrible.' I wondered whether these girls, who were comfortably off themselves, had a realistic notion of poverty and asked, 'do you think it matters to be very poor?' Emily echoed other children's views that a happy family was pivotal, rather than money itself. 'It matters to be poor if you don't have a family, if you have a family and you're poor it might be a bit better, because you won't be so unhappy...' though Harriet conceded, 'money is quite important for the food level, but not for like buying cars and stuff.'

Shakira included 'your valuables' among things that were important to her, but she was clear about where material goods came in the hierarchy. She imagined that some people might put valuables at the top of their list but was adamant that family, friends and environment must all come above them. Linda and Shakira theorised that male violence and alienation from society was a result of not being able to earn one's living. Shakira said, ' I think there's mostly boys who are bad... there's been so many, I only know one woman. And every time I look on the news there's always a man who's done something, all of the time and when I see things...' Linda interrupted her, 'and I think most women don't like being bad, I think, but most men... they have got nothing else to do. They can't get jobs or anything, so they might just as well kill people.'

Begging, poverty, homelessness and children's solutions

Beggars were common around both schools and children referred to them regularly. The children associated poverty, begging and homelessness but had limited ideas about breaking the cycle. Most children were only concerned with local poverty, though a few talked about third-world poverty, discussed later in this chapter.

Akosua (Y3) was one of the children who talked about the relationship between poverty, absence of choices and the necessity of support from the council. She had been telling me how upset her granny had been when children had mocked her about 'her messy hair', and taunted that 'she lived on the road'. She explained the connections between poverty and looking 'messy' with impeccable logic. 'Sometimes people who live on the streets, sometimes have messy hair, but just because someone's got messy hair, it doesn't mean that they're poor.' Though my own follow-up question was clumsy, Akosua's story provides an example of the kind of material teachers might follow through on to explore issues of citizenship, inequality and social justice. 'Do you think people who are living on the streets, do you think they really have lots of money, and they've chosen to be on the street, or what?' I asked, trying to find out how far Akosua had a structural explanation of homelessness, in which people might be trapped into the poverty cycle.

Akosua replied: 'No, they haven't got no money, because they can't afford it [to live in a house]. But the council want money from them. But I mean how can they pay the council, when they haven't no money? Well, they well... they can only go to the bank if they need some money...' 'But you see Akosua,' I explained, crudely avoiding mention of loans, 'banks won't *give* you money, they will only give you money that you've already put in. They're giving you your own money. So what might the poor people do, do you think?' Akosua felt this was still the council's responsibility, 'They should go to the council. The council might find them like a little council house.'

Gulsen had apparently been mulling over Akosua's opinions and said she wanted to talk about poor people. Her view of poverty was tied closely to her fear of 'strangers' and people who might harm you (which she had talked about earlier) and this interfered with compassion or concern to remedy the situation. 'I don't think you should mix with poor people' she said, 'because they might be a bit strange, because they don't know much about other people... because they live on the street, and no one like really tells them anything, because they think, some people think they do look quite horrible...' Akosua, however, stuck with her more charitable interpretation, 'What's important about people,' she said, ' is that people need houses and stuff. They need everything... not like everything in the world, but they *need* things, they need milk... things that are good for you.'

Like Akosua, Sean used the concept of 'need' to talk about poverty. Assia and he talked about the tramps and beggars round the Pankhurst Estate. Assia's mum gave money to tramps and drunk people if they knocked at the door, though Assia thought they should have to spend their money on clothes and food, and not on beer. Sean's reply, 'the man needs help, he needs to get a house. I would give them all houses, all the people [living] on the street,' suggests that he identified poverty and homelessness as the root cause of social problems. Assia was much more hard-nosed about alcoholism. 'He uses the money for beer, it makes him sick. The police tries to help the drunk man, but he goes away.'

Children's theories feed into their fears about their own future, and they are disempowered from considering potential solutions to poverty. Opportunities are there, but not taken, to make links with some of the PSHE issues which lie at the heart of family breakdown which can then lead to poverty. Alcoholism and drug addiction are two of the conditions that destroy families and interfere with the ability to work productively. There are opportunities to link responsible sexual behaviour to reduce unwanted pregnancies with children's concerns about going into care and perhaps ultimately finding themselves on the streets. We could follow the lead the children themselves offer by practising joined-up thinking about health, sex and drugs education and poverty.

Edward and Abdul (9 year olds) talked about poverty and the need to share resources, a virtue they were taught at home. Though there were intimations that neither family was well-off, both boys were learning that other people's poverty was their responsibility. When I asked who should do something about poor people, Edward replied, 'It should be everyone.' Though he believed people should share wealth and land, at a personal level he conceded it was hard to share. His example was pragmatic. 'It's tempting, when you're at home, to just say no.' Abdul agreed: 'I don't want to share my peas and chips with my brothers, cos I'm hungry.' Edward explained 'there has to be a good reason not to share, like if you're really starving, and you haven't eaten. Some people disagree. They are people who are greedy. Their parents must teach them.' Abdul, however, reduced this basically socialist approach to individual handouts. 'Like when there's people begging, my mum gives money to them, and my dad.' Edward's parents also gave money to beggars. 'When she's driving from church, a man was asking for some money, like 50p, so he could go on a bus, and we were stopping and she would have given him 50p, but we couldn't stop because the lights changed. She said she would have just thrown 50p to him.'

Difficult though it may be for concerned and compassionate people to walk past a beggar without giving – and some religions, particularly Islam, regard giving to the needy as a religious duty – there are simple economic and social reasons why it is more effective to support a charity than give individual handouts. Charities like Shelter, the Salvation Army and Red Cross, which are concerned with poverty and homelessness, are anxious to point this out. Could children discuss this? I think so.

As reports based on empirical research from the charities and faith organisations show, the cause of much homelessness is family breakdown, children coming out of care without support, poor mental and physical health, alcoholism. No one individual can provide the systematic, thought-through programmes of support and rehabilitation needed to break these cycles. Moreover, organisations which can buy buildings to be renovated, set up social housing schemes, food kitchens, counselling services, refuges and training can take advantage of economies of scale which are out of individual reach.

Eight year old Nicholas and Alex, the sons of an architect and journalist respectively, talked about changes they would like in their neighbourhood. These issues had not been discussed at school, but they may have been discussed at home. The different levels of understanding and knowledge the two boys have about the world of money and economics is evident from the interview. Nicholas' ideas for change and powers of logic are impressive and indicate the level of debate that is possible even with quite young children and also how other children can be moved on by listening to what a friend has to say. Before we changed to a new topic, Alex said that he now thought he agreed with what Nicholas said, rather than holding to his own view about poverty.

The boys said they would like to see some of the old broken-down houses and empty buildings knocked down or converted into cinemas or cafés. Initially, they said they wanted more cafés to provide more food in the area. I thought they meant that there were not enough cafés and restaurants already, but Nicholas said no, it was because poor people were not getting enough food. His plan involved successful ventures subsidising the costs of charitable eating places and also grouping shops so that there would be more incentive for people to come. Cafés on their own were not the solution, he thought, 'because they might not have enough money ... but I think

I'd make it good for the cafés, because if we pick some cafés which are already out there, then they'll get a bit more money, and we could make some shops where things are cheaper for people, poor people, like you could get something for 10p. Something to eat for 10p.'

Less aware of the reality of economics than Nicholas, and revealing his confusion about the source of money and its relationship to payment for goods and services, Alex's idea of philanthropy was 'to make cafés only for poor people, with food that costs nothing at all.'

'Really a free place completely, where you give away food?' I asked.

'Yes'.

'And who would run these cafés?'

'Us.'

' And where would we get the money from, for all the food?'

'Sell cars,' said Alex.

'So we'd have to do a job to give the money to the café. What about the poor people, would it be OK just for them always to be just taking everything for free, or would they need to do anything?'

Alex now drew on Nicholas' proposal for subsidised food: 'Well, when they took something, when they take some food, the café will just give them some money.'

'You would give them some money? All the poor people who haven't got a lot of money, whose fault is it that they've got no money?' I asked.

Nicholas answered by developing his idea of subsidy, which was not too far removed from social security benefits. 'It's not really anybody's fault that they haven't got any money,' he said. '... I'd make them a bank and a bank [which] doesn't really look after people's money, but only poor people are allowed to go there, and have special bank cards that they put in the machine, and the bank'll give them some money. They don't need to put money in the bank to take it out.'

'You say it's not really anybody's fault. How does it happen then, that some people get too poor?' I asked.

Alex leapt in with his explanation, 'The burglars. It's the fault of the burglars ... they jump out and get all their money.'

'So you think that all the people you see who are really poor, they used to have some money, and they got burgled? Is that what you think as well Nicholas?'

But Nicholas made clear connections between unemployment, poverty and homelessness. 'No. Well they can't really find a job, so they don't know what to do, and if they haven't got a job, they haven't got enough money to have a house.'

Probing whether Nicholas saw unemployment in terms of personal blame or absence of opportunities, I asked: 'Right, Do you think they wanted to have a job, and if there was a job they would go and do it, or not?' But he replied, 'If there was a job that they could get, then they'd go and do it.'

Akosua and Gulsen's ideas about poverty and the reasons for it also developed from a discussion about changes they would like in their environment outside school and the amount of litter which spoiled public spaces for other people. They started to talk about the Queen, whom they regarded as one of the most privileged people in society. Interestingly, their objections to monarchy were related to wealth, but they also appeared to feel insulted and marginalised at a personal level. Drawing on fairy-tale imagery, they believed the queen was a spoiled, over-privileged woman who stayed in bed, owned everything including the land they lived on, and took no interest in the hardships of their lives.

Akosua said, 'Well it's not fair, because if there's rubbish everywhere, its not fair for them to do it ... you shouldn't throw stuff on the floor, because it's naughty and it isn't your land.'

'Whose land is it?' I asked.

'It's God's and maybe it's the Queen's.'

This triggered a line of reasoning about privilege, hierarchy and inequality. Akosua continued, 'Well I think the Queen should be banned from wearing crowns and jewellery dresses ... she's got everything, and when the old people die ... she doesn't go the cemetery and stuff.'

'Does she not?' I commented neutrally.

Akosua said, 'She stays in bed, eating stuff.'

Gulsen indicated that in her view, caring and charity from wealthy people were connected, 'Well the Queen is rich, yea, she don't care about the people who are dying. Cos she doesn't care, cos she doesn't give ... and the people are dying, yea, they feel sorry for themselves, because they don't want to die, because they want to spend their life still...' Akosua wanted to see tangible evidence of the monarchy's compassion and care, 'Like she doesn't have to give the jewellery to people, she can at least go to the cemetery and plant some flowers on there.'

'Akosua,' I asked, 'you said you thought the land belonged to the Queen. Do you want it to stay belonging to the Queen, or is that something you want to change?'

Gulsen butted in, 'I don't think it's fair, all of us, whoever lives in this country, I want them to own it.'

'How will we share it out do you think?' I asked.

Gulsen's solution was well short of complete abolition of inequality, but involved people with immense privilege, like the Queen, paying their own way. 'The Queen can live in a big house, I don't care about that, but she should be in charge of the houses, she should pay the bills and stuff, because she's the one who invents houses and stuff.'

Akosua's solution to poverty hints at principles of Keynesian theory, which recommends making money available for people to spend, in order to stimulate the economy. 'You should share the money,' she commented. ' Spend it, whoever's not spending their money, or like share their money ... they're poor because they can't have nothing. If they don't know what [they should use] to spend with, they're going to be poor, so they should really spend it when they grow up.' It is not clear whether Akosua believed that the wealthy should subsidise the poor through their spending; perhaps she means 'sharing' where she says 'spending' and her failure to differentiate who 'they' are makes interpretation difficult, but she could possibly, with help, understand the connection between public spending, demand and a strong economy.

'The sharing,' I asked, 'do you think everybody should have the same amount, or should some people have more than other people?'

Contradicting her earlier view about the Queen keeping her wealth, Gulsen joined Akosua in chorusing 'the same amount'. 'Everybody? You don't mind?' I pressed.

'Yeh, whoever they are,' answered Akosua.

Janine and Rehana had been learning about rationing during the Second World War and were not sure how it worked. 'There were a number of days when people would buy whatever they wanted,' Rehana said. I asked what they thought of this way of organising things, in the war. 'I think it was good', Rehana said, 'so everybody had the same thing, and some people couldn't show off cos they had more.' Janine thought that the ration books meant that they didn't have money, but Rehana understood that this was a way of ensuring fair play and declared: 'I think everybody should have the same amount of food, not less than others, and not more than others.' Now the war was over, they both felt having money and a choice of what you could buy was a preferable situation.

The problem of scammers

In contrast to this discourse of charity, equity and sharing, some children revealed that they understood that there were dilemmas of working out who was in genuine need, and who was cheating the system. Edward said, 'Some poor people are scamming, asking for money. Some people are using them [ie charitable people]. I knew they were doing it, but they said they'd beat me up if I told on them. They said I was lying about it.' Honesty in the face of others' dishonesty was problematic in much the same way as was intervening when other people were getting hurt. Toyin had witnessed theft from shops but had not been able to do anything about it, because she was threatened. Farzana commented that people sold the things they stole but that 'you really can't do something like go to the police, because you may get hurt, you may meet the person again, and they know it was you, cos you were the only person who knew.'

Poverty and Human Rights

Contemporary analyses identify poverty as the root cause of failure to meet the majority of human rights requirements. Article 25 of the Declaration on Human Rights, for example, states that everyone has the right to a standard of living adequate for the health and well-being of himself (sic) and his family including food, clothing, housing and medical care, necessary social services, and the right to security in the event of disability, widowhood, old age or other lack of livelihood in circumstances beyond his control. Article 27 of the Convention on the Rights of the Child gives children the right to a standard of living adequate for her/his physical, mental, spiritual, moral and social development. It might feel as if one is peeling an endless onion, constantly revealing a new issue in the effort to get to the core of problems. However, to recognise that economic and social inequality lie at the heart of the children's concerns provides us – and them – with the tools to understand and ultimately change things. Simplistic approaches to poverty, inequality or family difficulties which personalise and blame are disingenuous.

The first part of this chapter about the value of money suggests that children were drawing on a discourse about the minimum resources that people need and are entitled to, if they are to have a reasonable quality of life, as opposed to excessive luxury. Underlying the discussion about people on the street are assumptions about the nature of resource distribution in society, welfare provision and, for some children, the availability of work. As Francesca in Y6 and Nicholas in Y3 both pointed out, a person who is in work will be in a position to afford a place to live and pay the bills. An unemployed person in the twenty-first century will expect to draw on a variety of social security benefits to maintain a minimum standard of living.

The context for such debate could be the history curriculum in Key Stage 2, working from either the Victorian unit or Britain since the 1930s. The idea that no one was owed or should expect a certain standard of living as of right would have been familiar in the middle of the nineteenth century and was still prevalent at the time of the depression in the early 1930s. Charity and punitive workhouses existed in the Victorian period for those needy and indigent people who fell by the wayside, but it took the welfare interventions of the twentieth century and particularly post-World War Two to guarantee a minimum level of economic security for the young, the old, the sick, the unemployed.

Then there are issues about who is unemployed and why. An individualised, personalised discourse operates on the assumption that the work is there and that some people choose to scrounge and scam rather than knuckle down. This was Edward's view, though Nicholas considers the availability of work. The approach in the material produced by NGOs like Oxfam and Save the Children is to start with inequalities all round us in Britain, before moving on to global inequality. Society values some occupations by means of high pay and claims to value others (such as child care) without making adequate financial recompense. Links could be made with global issues and the ways in which work options and redundancies link to the international economy and decisions by multinationals about where to locate their factories. There are questions about the vast differentials between rates of pay for different services in society and the exploitation of the most vulnerable in the workplace, for example asylum seekers and immigrants forced to accept poor wages. Again, there are opportunities for children to begin to understand global connections – themes which I develop in Chapter 7.

Poverty in other countries

In this book I have not so far tried to track individual children's attitudes and contributions across a range of issues. The discussion of poverty is an exception, since in all the hours of interviewing, only three children raised concerns about poverty elsewhere in the world. Like many other children, all three had views about poverty at home as well. These three made connections where others did not, and perhaps this suggests something about teacher intervention and curriculum development.

Akosua, who talked about her mother being left short of money when her father left, and who thought the council should provide homes for the homeless, said 'I'm worried about the world ... the way that people are treated, like they're treated like flies and everything, and they haven't got nothing to eat, and like some people are rich and they don't even spend money, and the people who are poor, and I don't even like that about the world, I'm worried about whatever's going to happen, like I think it's gonna be bad.'

Emily and Harriet from Y4, who felt that wealthy people should give to beggars, also had a conscience about poverty in the developing world, which they saw as the responsibility of the rich. One of their teachers who had a personal commitment to the issues of global inequality had suggested that they could do something. This was the only example in the transcripts in which children introduced practical ideas about how to become involved with the developing world. I am struck by the detail of the human story which had gained their attention as well as the focus on supporting self-help projects.

Emily said, 'Like India, and like poor parts of India, cos some [people/countries] are rich, quite rich, and they haven't got much food, and the crops won't grow sometimes, and I feel quite bad about that, because we could do something about it, like ... send packages of food over, and now they're starting making wells, and we're doing a cake stall at school.'

Harriet: 'Our head said we could, and we're going to do a cake stall, and with all the money, we're going to get about £40 and we're going to send it ... off to Africa, wasn't it? So they can ... with the money they can get a well there, so they don't have to walk as far. Yeah, Barbara (a teacher) was telling us how far they had to walk to get water, ten miles, no it was fourteen miles, just to get one bottle of water, and they have to carry it all on their head, really we decided to make a cake stall.'

Endangered species, the environment, animals

I have suggested that one should take note of what people don't choose to talk about as well as what they do. There are two notable and important characteristics of the majority of children's conversations relevant to the issues in this section:

- they talked about issues very close to home and appeared to have little knowledge or interest in issues further away

- children who themselves introduced concerns about issues remote from their personal lives tended to be concerned about the environment and endangered species rather than about other human beings.

These are some examples:

Emily and Harriet talked about global poverty but when it came to listing the things most important to them, animals, not people, came top of the list. Both watched animal programmes, including Animal Hospital, on television and were angry about people killing tigers and whales and endangered species. Emily was particularly incensed about animals being killed just for sport and the fun of it. Harriet was upset that some people were cruel to their pets and gave vivid details. Jo and Derek worried about big cats and bears being shot for their fur and were saddened that pets were put down on Animal Hospital. Jo wanted to put his dogs at the top of his list of important things, along with his family.

One of Gulsen's own questions was about whether one should kill animals for food, and she and Akosua got into an argument about this. Both agreed that one shouldn't kill animals for fun, but Akosua didn't eat meat and thought they shouldn't be killed for food either. In the pretend-argument game, with me playing devil's advocate to get them to justify their opinions, I argued that it was alright to kill animals: after all they didn't have feelings like people. But Akosua was adamant that wild animals did have feelings. 'Imagine if you was a tiger or something,' she cried, 'and someone killed you, you wouldn't like it.' Shakira reasoned that care for the environment must come before material values – 'before valuables, because some people cut down trees ... and they don't think about themselves and if someone else is going to die because of there is no trees.'

These examples are not atypical of children this age. Work on endangered species and the environment is written into the science and the geography national curricula in KS 2 and the topic is popular with children and teachers. But I think it is problematic that there is no equivalent awareness and concern about human lives. Children might debate whether human lives have at least equivalent value to endangered animals and trees. This is not a zero-sum situation where concern for the environment and animals cancels out or 'uses up' the available compassion for people. Children don't lack concern and empathy but the curriculum is sadly deficient in bringing these issues into the overt curriculum and harnessing children's concern for justice, particularly for other children. Children who can feel for pets and wild animals far away, in pain or at risk, can feel for human beings in similar circumstances too. The difference is probably that animals are seen as innocent victims of human cruelty and greed – but this could be precisely where children could start making connections with poverty in the wider world.

Education for economic and social understanding

If my analysis about poverty and social justice is correct, empathy and personal tolerance will be only part of an effective intervention strategy. That so many children perform verbal violence against one another, using their parents' real or imagined economic insecurity as the weapon, suggests they have internalised the message that poverty or lack of work are individual failings and that if people simply tried harder and were better at managing their money, no-one would be clothed from a charity shop. If people could just learn to be nicer to one another – not argue and fight and chuck each other out *in extremis* – there would be no homelessness.

The implicit ideology of PSHE/Citizenship guidance confirms this individualistic analysis. It emphasises looking after your money (with an eye to future wants and needs and saving) and understanding about differential resource allocation and economic choices. This seems to be the recipe for success in an idealised middle-class world, where there are no inequalities in society or cycles of poverty and where lack of work is just a matter of individual fecklessness. The material I obtained during the interviews suggests that some children, at least, were capable of handling ideas that the school curriculum did not tap into.

Many people have accepted that pleas to be nice do not get to the root of racism and that children need to have a sense of the long history of inequality and exploitation that underlies it, if there are to be real improvements. My argument about the necessity for genuine education about economic and social inequality has a similar basis. Historically, other than the changes brought about through technological development, there are two major ways in which improvements and changes in society come about. One is through war and the other is through organised, informed political action. Presumably we do not hope for war. Unless one believes that the only solutions to our unequal society are handouts, a little voluntary work and refraining from being unnecessarily abusive, it is difficult to see how the current educational agenda can lead to children understanding enough about their society to change it through informed action.

6

The making of citizens

Values in society are controversial. Values in education are even more so... [they] structure the very structure of the education system, its institutions and practices. (Taylor, 1998:5)

This chapter is about values in citizenship education, and hence values in a democracy. The 'Values, Aims and Purposes of Education' statements at the beginning of the National Curriculum document, to be monitored through OFSTED, are intended to permeate a curriculum which is 'children's entitlement'. I interpret this entitlement in line with Bruner's philosophy that education must be 'not only a process that transmits culture, but also one that provides alternative views of the world and strengthens the will to explore them' (1979:117). Accordingly, this chapter offers ideas for a curriculum which empowers teachers and children to explore alternative views of the world, so that you can design material for yourselves and do more than implement a ready-made set of activities.

Despite the emphasis in material for the primary age range on developing personal morality and interpersonal relationships, there is little clarification about the links with the wider world of citizenship; this is what I will attempt to make explicit here, starting with the diagram overleaf.

Values Education and Values In Education

The guidelines on implementing the PSHE/Citizenship guidance in primary schools (QCA, 2000) emphasise the necessity for a whole school ethos and approach, over and above the statements in the

HOW SELF-ESTEEM AND SELF-CONFIDENCE RELATE TO CITIZENSHIP IN THE LOCAL, NATIONAL AND GLOBAL COMMUNITIES

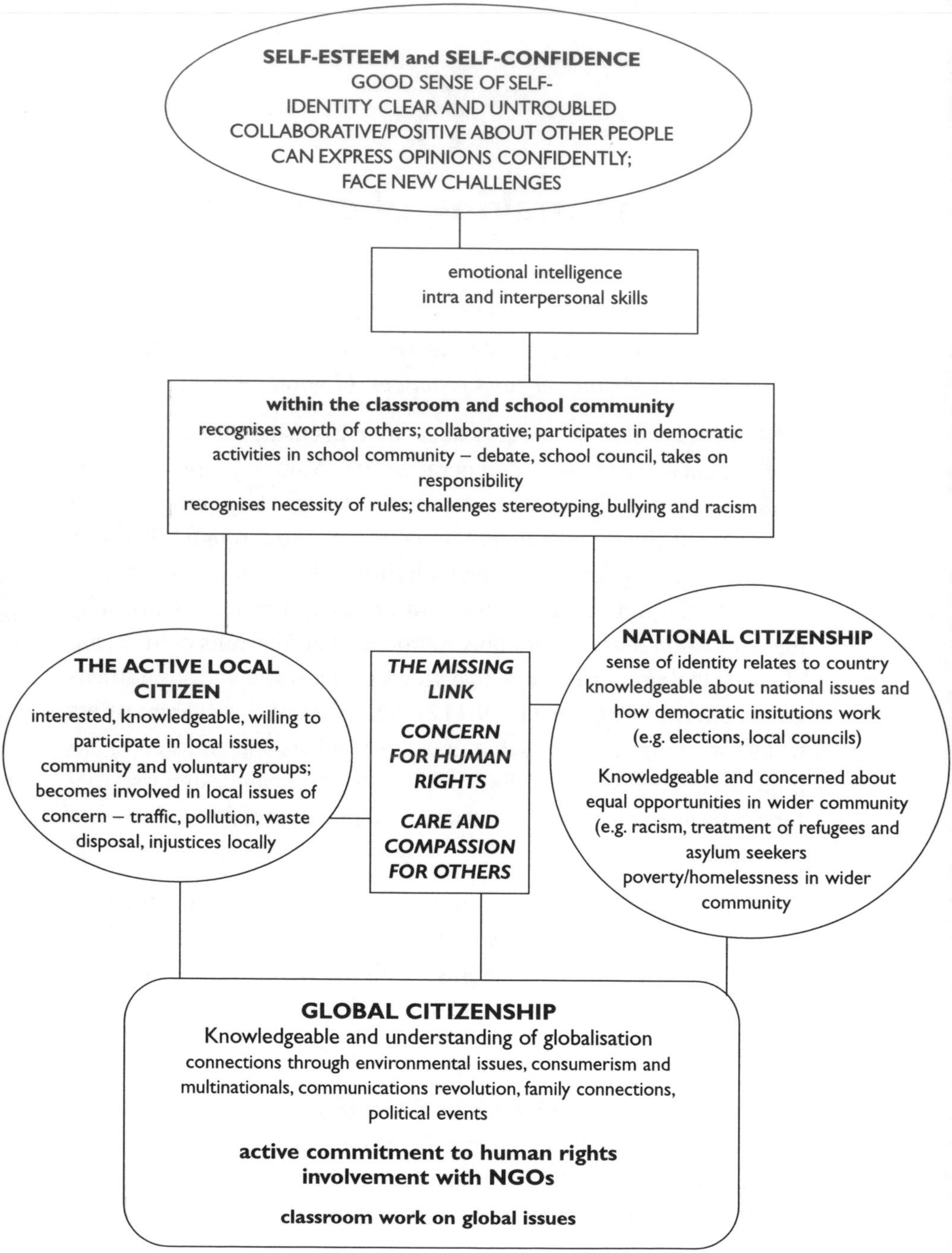

SELF-ESTEEM and SELF-CONFIDENCE
GOOD SENSE OF SELF-
IDENTITY CLEAR AND UNTROUBLED
COLLABORATIVE/POSITIVE ABOUT OTHER PEOPLE
CAN EXPRESS OPINIONS CONFIDENTLY;
FACE NEW CHALLENGES
emotional intelligence
intra and interpersonal skills
within the classroom and school community
recognises worth of others; collaborative; participates in democratic activities in school community – debate, school council, takes on responsibility
recognises necessity of rules; challenges stereotyping, bullying and racism
THE ACTIVE LOCAL CITIZEN
interested, knowledgeable, willing to participate in local issues, community and voluntary groups; becomes involved in local issues of concern – traffic, pollution, waste disposal, injustices locally
THE MISSING LINK
CONCERN FOR HUMAN RIGHTS
CARE AND COMPASSION FOR OTHERS
NATIONAL CITIZENSHIP
sense of identity relates to country
knowledgeable about national issues and how democratic insitutions work
(e.g. elections, local councils)
Knowledgeable and concerned about equal opportunities in wider community
(e.g. racism, treatment of refugees and asylum seekers
poverty/homelessness in wider community
GLOBAL CITIZENSHIP
Knowledgeable and understanding of globalisation
connections through environmental issues, consumerism and multinationals, communications revolution, family connections, political events
active commitment to human rights
involvement with NGOs
classroom work on global issues

Guidance. The values of the school, demonstrated and lived out in every part of its relationships and practices, will be the test of its commitment to citizenship education.

'Values Education' is the generic name for spiritual, moral, social and cultural education, development education, religious education, multicultural and antiracist education and, above all, Human Rights education which underpins concepts of a good citizen and a just society. The boundaries between private life and public life, where citizenship is conventionally thought to belong, are fuzzy. As some of the transcripts have shown, it is not always easy in practice to draw the boundary lines between private and public ethics and values – presenting a challenge to teachers with assumptions about unproblematic common values. Compulsory religious education in a multi-faith society, with Christianity as the central plank, is particularly pertinent to a discussion of values, since for many people their value system is intimately linked with their religious beliefs, which may not be 'broadly Christian'.

Attempts by government to manage values in society through the school curriculum are not new. Throughout the nineteenth century in Britain, as industrialisation and urbanisation took hold and suffrage for working men was extended, ideologies about 'civilising the masses' through education and religion were quite explicit. Many people regard what is happening in schools now as not just educationally prescriptive but as transparent social control. You will have your own view about the role and place of the national literacy and numeracy strategies and SATs.

Accepting that one's interpretation reveals one's own value systems, the Values, Aims and Purposes Statement in the National Curriculum is potentially far more radical then the PSHE/Citizenship guidance itself, going beyond tolerance of diversity, knowledge and understanding, and proposing for education the goals of 'enabl(ing) pupils to think creatively and critically, ... solv(ing) problems and ... mak(ing) a difference for the better... (with) the opportunity to become creative, innovative, enterprising and capable of leadership ... for their future lives as workers and citizens' (QCA, 2000:11). The connections are established between developing a sense of identity, equality of opportunity, a healthy and just democracy, a productive economy and sustainable development. The Statement asserts that education should enable children to respond positively to opportunities and challenges in a world of economic, social and cultural change. It is made clear that education should have more than a conservative purpose of passing on 'enduring values' and prepare children to be responsible and caring citizens, capable of contributing to the development of a just society by developing their integrity and autonomy (ibid: 13). This implies that education should have a progressive agenda which would equip children to critique the society they live in and become familiar with contemporary discourses and explanations about inequality so they can develop a range of ideas about solutions.

Appreciating alternative readings of values is important for democracy and for citizenship education, because these profoundly affect what teachers might aim to achieve. An influential paper in 1992 by the philosopher T. McGoughlin introduced the distinction – now regularly used within the literature about citizenship – between a 'minimalist' and a 'maximalist' model of citizenship education. The former is limited to children learning about public duty and representative processes, and is based on conformity to existing rules of law and order. The latter is about developing critical faculties, an understanding and knowledge of issues related to equality and justice on a local, societal and global scale. Thus it is about empowerment, in which children learn to take responsibility for their own lives, and learn how they can influence and participate, not just through conforming but also through their vision of a better world. What follows is an exploration of both practice and value in implementing a maximalist agenda.

Learning democracy through 'doing democracy'

Teachers know that they can't force pupils to take on their ideas. Those who disagree are not likely to change their minds. They may well resent you and ignore you in other contexts, even if they defer to your power at the time. This can be the fate of such school values as 'don't fight', as earlier chapters have illustrated. Moreover, you don't learn to ride a bike by reading the manual: taking on the values of citizenship can only occur through *doing* citizenship, as an active participating citizen of the school. Schools in which children are bullied by autocratic adults, herded, ordered around, shouted at and shown no respect are unlikely to achieve their goals of instilling democratic ideas, and cannot claim to be providing opportunities for experiencing citizenship. Ironically, the very schools that have lovely displays celebrating children's strengths may be those that counteract the messages with authoritarian approaches to behaviour management.

Democratic societies in which all are equal citizens operate through mutual respect and are neither authoritarian nor dogmatic. They offer possibilities for raising one's own concerns, for debate and conflict resolution. Schools' Councils are important but not sufficient, because although children may elect their representatives, not every child can experience the School Council itself. Anyway, there is plenty of anecdotal evidence that many School Councils are less democratic in practice than in rhetoric. In class, the ethos of democracy needs to translate into co-operative work in the ordinary classroom setting, debates, circle time and role-play. Circle time can be used not just for building self-esteem and tolerance but also as a vehicle to teach children how to conduct discussions about issues that have relevance to a broad citizenship agenda. A number of organisations are producing specialist material and ideas to this end (see Chapter 8: Resources Section).

Active engagement with issues and feeling that you can make a difference

'Doing citizenship' implies that you are working from or developing a set of values about the way society works and relationships within it. Many children will learn this at home, but the school also has a role and that is to provide a context in which values are explored. This will partly happen through the hidden curriculum – the classroom and school ethos – but will also be explicit whenever children discuss what they mean by a just and fair society, what they see as their relationship with a wider society – including a global society – and what kind of responsibility they should take on.

'Doing citizenship' implies that you are actively involved in issues and feel you can make a difference through your participation. This may be within the school or it may be within the wider community. It follows that the curriculum should incorporate issues which are real to the children, which need debate and decision making and a follow-through with action. Secondary schools are sometimes better at this – and not just because their pupils are older. It's more to do with the analysis of active citizenship in a democracy which acknowledges the variety of ways in which power is negotiated, obstructed or influenced. As the previous chapters have made clear, primary age children have a great many issues on their minds and know about many things which are directly relevant to their development as citizens. These can and should be the issues that are brought into school.

To illustrate what I mean, here are two stories, both true, both coming from children's active engagement in a local issue in which they genuinely hoped to make a difference. Each scenario has implications for children's understanding about how democracy works in a local community and their own ultimate sense of agency, but the messages delivered by the two activities are poles apart.

Scenario 1: As part of a geography project on the local environment, Y5 children engaged in a local consultation process to determine the future use of a piece of land. They did a survey of how people in the community would prefer the land to be developed, using some of the proposals already available from the council. They also canvassed views within the school community. With respect to the wider community, they didn't do much more than tap into existing opinions, some organised more locally than others, but they ended up believing that the majority of people in the school community and in the local vicinity did not want another supermarket, as there were already three. They wrote to the council with an outline of their survey and its results. They got back a patronising, if polite, letter letting them know that the decision had already been taken at council level for another supermarket to be built. Result: deflated, disempowered and cynical children, possibly infected with the seeds of apathy, which contemporary politicians find so alarming. Looking back, it would seem that this project was never more than a curriculum 'game', never going beyond some of the elements in the geography programme of study. This was largely due to the limited way in which the approach was conceptualised.

Scenario 2: This story comes from a secondary school, but primary teachers might think about the issues here, rather than whether an exactly equivalent project would be viable. (I am not sure it would be.) I think this second group of children was learning about the real ways in which one can influence decisions.

For many months the school, which has a pokey playground backing onto railway arches and derelict ground, had been petitioning the council to release the land to extend their playground. The pupils invited councillors into the school, they organised petitions, they went to council meetings and were bored rigid by the procedures. Nothing happened. Frustrated but not ready to give up, they started to work out how many votes were represented in the school – not their own, since no pupils were of voting age – but in the wider community of which they were a part (parents/carers, friends). Of their own accord and out of school, they started to approach potential councillors, pointing out that they, as constituents, wanted to know their attitude to the arches and the derelict land, and making clear that in their families, votes would be cast according to this issue. Near election time a leading councillor came to the school to talk to the Head. The pupils apparently knew who he was, though what happened next was definitely not set up or premeditated. It appears that two boys came to the Head's office to report that they were being excluded for fighting in the playground. Realising who the visitor was they turned to him and said: 'This has happened because our playground is inadequate. We would not be fighting if we had proper space. We intend to go to the press and tell them that the council is not interested in us having a decent playground, even though there are no plans for the land to be used for something else.' They also reminded the councillor of their research about the potential voting power of people in their community who supported them. Apparently the important councillor promptly took out his mobile phone, made a call, and the stalemate was resolved.

There are lessons here about being 'real' with children about how democracy works. They need to understand that interest groups can capture the agenda, that votes have to be canvassed, that there is power in the media and, as the next chapter discusses, that economic considerations rather than wish-lists govern democratic decisions. They need adults who have an analysis of political action that includes an understanding of power and empowerment. These issues are not remote from children's lives, even in primary school. We need to help children make the conceptual links, so that they look for and start to understand the ways in which power is organised, used (and abused) and the options and limits of available action within a democracy. This can and should start within the school, for example with attention to bullying and anti-bullying policies. It can then move into the wider community, so that children become involved in, say, regeneration schemes for their estates, or community projects with respect to the environment. As the previous chapters indicated, such ideas are within even the youngest children's interest and intellectual capacity.

The skills of active participation in a democratically run community

'Having a voice' – the skills to participate effectively

Doing citizenship implies that you have the personal confidence and skills to organise your ideas, to talk in public, to listen and debate rationally. It also means that you will have learned to expect rational, evidence-based argument, and that you won't be content with knee-jerk responses. 'Having a voice' is more than that: it entails planning the curriculum to enhance children's opportunities to argue and debate issues, learn how to evaluate different points of view including the manipulative views coming from the media, and to develop skills of advocacy, arbitration and mediation. This kind of work need not be restricted to RE, drama or circle time. There are possibilities right across the curriculum, since opinions and perspectives, attitudes and values are part of every subject in their wider sense. It is possible to go well beyond the advice in documentation from the QCA (eg QCA 2000: *History Teacher's Guide Update*). Opportunities within History are generally undervalued and under-used.

Doing history (as I have written elsewhere, Claire, 1996) involves the marshalling of arguments and explanations, the ability to hold more than one possibility in one's mind, allow for multiple perspectives, and being able to communicate one's understanding.

Teaching thinking skills as part of developing active citizenship

Ideas about teaching thinking skills are not particularly new. In Scandinavia and some countries in Europe (such as Italy) children learn a formal subject called Rhetoric, in which they are taught how to debate in a structured way, giving them access to the formal rules of argument and logic. Critical thinking skills provide one with the ability to recognise false assumptions or conclusions based on inadequate or atypical data. These skills are needed to clarify values, test principles, distinguish between relevant and irrelevant information, expose assumptions, infer points of view. They are essential to people who need to argue their own case, discern the strengths and weaknesses of various proposals and be able to see through manipulative propaganda.

Philosophy for Children uses techniques of Socratic dialogue, often starting with stories, picture books or poems. It is an extraordinarily child-friendly and accessible way to develop children's powers of thinking. (See Chapter 8 for organisations and addresses.) Protagonists have disagreed over the context and transferability of such skills but recent work in Britain in curriculum subjects as different as art, science, English and geography have suggested that children who learn, practise and develop thinking skills in real contexts, rather than in isolation from issues they would be considering anyway, do transfer them to other contexts.

Michael Bonnett (1994) reminds us how learning to think connects to personal and social education and to the themes of citizenship discussed in this book. Learning and understanding do not mean having ideas planted in your head by someone else. To learn and understand means taking responsibility for your own thinking and being honest, responsible, open and reflexive about your values. A sense of your own worth and identity, the courage of your convictions, the confidence to question, take risks, face consequences and be constructively self-critical are crucial, and the quality of the relationship between pupils and teachers is central, not peripheral. Such is the approach embraced by Philosophy for Children.

Going beyond critical thinking to decision-making

So far I have referred to the important skills of debate and rational argument and the ways in which children can be helped to become critical thinkers. Citizenship requires more than this, because in the real world, decision-making is almost always both the purpose and the end of the process of considering issues, even if the decision is, on balance, to do nothing.

Decision-making does come into some programmes for teaching thinking to children, but it is seldom given systematic, dedicated attention in primary schools. One might wonder why it is so neglected, when the skills are essential, not just to adults but to any growing person. Think of the range of decisions one has to take – from trivial to major – what shall I wear today, where shall I go on holiday, shall I move house, shall I have a child, shall I have her inoculated for MMR? Children can be taught to think logically about small, manageable decisions in their own lives. Brunerian fashion, they can move to wider decisions and, as they mature, engage with decisions that need to be taken on behalf of other people in a local or national context. This is part of responsible citizenship as well as personal development.

The stages in decision-making

A decision that does not involve choice is no decision at all. Step 1 in decision-making is to be clear about the problem or issue to be decided, what it involves and what is not relevant. Step 2 is to consider the various alternative courses of action, including 'do nothing'.

Two important stages follow, involving value judgements and probability:

1. attach *values to the consequences* of each course of action and consider the values you hold about the processes that

will be involved (for instance you might value being chosen for the team, but feel that the effort involved in training is more than you can cope with)

2. consider the *likelihood of your preferred consequence*, or the potential unwanted consequences, actually happening (even if you train every evening you're unlikely to be selected; your homework will suffer.)

You are then in a position to weigh up the pros and cons of the different courses of action, and decide what to do, on the basis of

- what you want to happen (values)
- what is likely to happen (probability).

Here is a child-friendly example, to show how this works.

Alice is having a birthday party and drawing up her guest list. She definitely wants to invite her best friends, Femi and Shola. The problem is Eddie who doesn't get on with Femi, but who is close friends with Shola. Shola is bound to let him know about the party and both of them will be hurt and upset if Alice doesn't invite Eddie. So will both sets of parents, as they are good friends. So:

CHOICES	CONSEQUENCES	
	Good consequences	Bad consequences
Invite Eddie	Parents happy Shola happy Eddie happy	Eddie and Femi get into a fight and spoil the party
Don't invite Eddie	Eliminates chance of a fight Femi happy	Parents and Shola unhappy Eddie angry and hurt

The Carroll diagram shows that the decision is determined by how much Alice cares about the different consequences (her values) and how likely the fight is (probability). In formal adult decision-making people are asked to put numbers against their values and probabilities (eg.75% likelihood of a fight and 80% for the value placed on 'no fight') and then perform a mathematical calculation using a formula. But it would be sufficient for children to consider their values and probabilities using words (I care a lot about this; the likelihood is quite small) and set out possible strategies and solutions. This example was based on a real child's problem; she decided to invite 'Eddie' and asked both sets of parents to intervene if necessary.

In reality one would not go through the formal process to make a decision of this kind. The exercise is still worth doing, using children's own dilemmas or some problem related to the school or the community to give children plenty of experience of an approach which acknowledges feelings and encourages logical, rational problem-solving. For more serious and complicated decisions where it is necessary to keep track of a variety of options and potential consequences, the formal methods of decision analysis can be a powerful and empowering tool.

The ideas of Emotional Literacy

One of the bonuses of the new PSHE/Ct guidance is to confirm for teachers the importance of working with children's feelings and attitudes. Though teaching Thinking Skills is dominated by cognitive approaches, both Philosophy for Children and emotional literacy make links between thinking and feeling. In the wake of Goleman's (1996) best-seller, *Emotional Intelligence,* little empires have grown up rapidly, with different protagonists producing rationales and resources in support of their particular approaches. Much of the theory of emotional literacy is familiar: it emphasises high self-esteem and being in touch with one's own feelings as part of motivation to work at a task, manage one's own behaviour, listen to and work effectively with others. The difference between now and twenty to thirty years ago is that programmes are being evaluated to test the correlation between their success and other variables such as academic success (SATs), reduction in behaviour problems and truancy at school.

Although not trying to create a therapeutic community in the classroom, the various programmes for emotional literacy have particular resonance for teachers who find that the possibility of rational debate about issues is undermined by the emotional instability and behavioural difficulties of some children. Emotional literacy is aimed at developing self-awareness and, through the ability to understand oneself, to move through and beyond the blocks to personal effectiveness and development. Some programmes emphasise teaching teachers first to listen to children and acknowledge the ways in which their own buttons can be pressed, before they move to helping children to become better listeners. Some put the main burden on 'feelings' which can be harnessed to support tolerance of diversity. Others discuss the importance of emotionally literate people for a safe and sensitive response to management issues in the school, including bullying. Others again emphasise the importance of trusting relationships and mutual respect in creating a community which nurtures dialogue, critical thought and moral reasoning.

Advocates of emotional literacy claim that children develop an openness to ideas which stimulates imagination, creativity and a sense of being empowered to make things happen. The voices in this book are testimony to the many anxieties and negative emotions that children have to deal with. Circle time has been the chief vehicle for fostering emotional literacy in the primary classroom and for encouraging discussion of difficult issues round family relationships, anxieties about sexuality and the future, or drugs education. But it is probably far too public a forum for highly vulnerable children to benefit personally and for them, other, more private areas of the curriculum may be preferable for the development of emotional literacy, for example, art, music, drama (particularly using puppets) and English (stories, poetry) focusing on feelings and conflict resolution.

Knowing and understanding about the issues – political literacy

The previous three sections discussed process, but there is a body of knowledge and understanding which is also part of citizenship education. Crick (1998) was concerned that children should understand how the democratic system in Britain works and this is part of the statutory requirements for Key Stage 3 and 4. In Key Stage 2 children are supposed to know why and how rules and laws are made and enforced, why different rules are needed in different situations and how to take part in making and changing rules. Such statements can be interpreted in local ways, so children debate and democratically agree classroom rules or decide in the School Council about rules for lunch hour. The challenge is how to take political literacy wider and, without being dreary and dry, give children a sense of agency in issues in the wider community. They may also need to learn hard lessons that democracy is full of fault lines, despite the unproblematic rhetoric that they be taught 'what democracy is, and about the basic institutions that support it locally and nationally'.

Learning to think about the issues means relating to the major concerns of their time and place. Some issues carry enormous emotional power, are highly politicised, and have potentially negative consequences for ordinary lives, for example, racist victimisation of individuals, the situation of asylum seekers threatened with deportation to their original countries, violent attacks by animal rights activists, even tube strikes. Anything that is on the news or discussed by adults is potentially within the knowledge of KS 2 children, even if never mentioned in school. It is not possible to think about such matters in a totally unemotional way. As Michael Bonnett (1994) pointed out, feelings are part and parcel of how we understand and know things, not separate from them.

An example of how emotional literacy interacts with political literacy came from a friend who told me that his eight year old had come back from school extremely upset about the trashing and barricading of a large house near their home. This house had been a squat for many years, and some of the children who lived there went to his child's school. The date was approaching when the squatters would be able to claim squatters' rights permanently; the owners of the house had evicted them and made the property absolutely uninhabitable. It turned out that my friend's daughter had been making disturbing connections. In her class were Kosovan refugees, and she knew that they had been burned out of their home during the war. 'Daddy', she asked, 'are we safe? Will our house get taken away from us?' Did the school take any of this on? I wondered. The answer was no.

It is a condition of rational dialogue, which moves beyond emotive and potentially knee-jerk reactions, to have information about what is actually happening, the arguments put by both sides, a sense of the alternatives, the possible consequences and the legal situation. This is why it is crucial that teachers have adequate knowledge about Human Rights, the Children's Rights legislation and amendments to the Race Relations Acts. This equips them to model how 'hard information' can make all the difference to the power of a debate.

Values in society: How do we decide what is just and right?

The child's anxiety about the business of the squatted house illustrates the impossibility of discussing local concerns without drawing on values and the nature of our relationships and responsibilities to one another. Many Key Stage 3 resources examine what we mean by a just and democratic society and Key Stage 2 teachers could easily adapt some of this material. The question of how to decide between different interests and values will soon come up. Cathie Holden's research (1999) suggested that primary teachers do not see issues of justice, right and wrong as problematic. They were confident that their own views were right and when children's ideas were contrary to theirs, tended to say that the parents who had introduced such conflicting ideas were wrong or that they did not have appropriate values. It is profoundly unhelpful and undemocratic to impose absolutist values on children growing up in a plural society and to deny them the opportunity to debate and justify what they mean by good and right attitudes and action.

Moral absolutism and moral relativism in a multicultural world

Moral absolutism and moral relativism in their extreme forms are at the opposite ends of a continuum, and we are not forced into either position. We can reject moral relativism without accepting that there is 'one truth' or that everyone knows and agrees about what is right (moral absolutism). Moral relativism implies that 'anything goes' and that it is impossible to challenge a value if it is rooted in the cultural traditions of some group. As the feminist philosopher Mary Midgley (1991) points out, there *are* boundaries to toleration in the case of both moral absolutism or moral relativism, demonstrated when human rights are transgressed. On the other hand, different communities and cultures do legitimately hold different values and this can undermine people's confidence in what they may or may not object to. Post-modernist perspectives criticise cultural and moral imperialism. They emphasise tolerance and relativism in the face of cultural diversity; the outcome is that some people may feel unable to take a stand against practices in 'another' culture, even when they seem to transgress important principles. The argument is that the value systems used to explain and judge cultural practices are themselves culturally specific, imbued with the implicit biases (white, male, bourgeois) of Western religion, philosophy and political economy. Hard-line post-modernist arguments can make it extremely difficult for an outsider to object to any cultural practice, since tradition and custom are enlisted to explain and justify the situation.

But post-modernist relativism is not the only philosophical position available to us. Most contemporary Human Rights literature notes that women's rights are central to a rights agenda across the world. Ironically, the result of moral relativism is to privilege an entrenched, conservative group – who may also have the power of male privilege – and to deny support to less powerful, often female groups who are struggling to emancipate themselves. This is made abundantly clear by black feminists such as Alice Walker and Pratibha Parma (condemning the practice of female genital mutilation) (Walker and Parmar 1993), and Rabbi Julia Neuberger in her critique of sexist orthodoxy within all the main religions and not just Judaism (Neuberger, 1995). The result is *powerfully conservative and anti-emancipatory* for any group that is struggling against oppressive practices within a specific culture.

Accepting practices in our own or another society on the grounds that we should not interfere, means that we will deny support to people who are trying to change this practice. The aphorism '*is does not imply ought*' reminds us that acknowledging or explaining a religious or cultural practice is not the same as justifying or recommending it. I can explain why it was common to deny girls a good education in 'my' (or someone else's) culture, or why Irish or Black people were subject to demeaning stereotypes, but this does not mean that I should accept these practices or use the explanations to justify their continuation. It is also important to remember that being an outsider isn't necessarily a bar to criticising, because as Parekh (2000) and Midgley (1991) remind us, cultures are not watertight. Within any community there are always sub-cultures which do not accept certain practices that other sub-cultures do uphold. The Parekh Report reminds us that people become trapped into a conservative past by terms like 'ethnic group' which deny diversity, difference and change within the group itself.

If we hold with human rights principles, we can't have it both ways. White South Africans who upheld apartheid claimed that no one 'who didn't live there' had the right to criticise the regime, and dismissed the anti-apartheid movement as partisan. Rightly, this did not stop the movement in its tracks. Sitting on the fence and refusing to make a judgement on human rights issues becomes poignant and paradoxical when you think about Governor Wallace's actions in Alabama in the 1960s, Ken SaroWiwa's stand against environmental destruction in Nigeria in 1998, or the Taliban's restrictions on women in Afghanistan, imposed in 2000.

We live in a society with a number of agreed values about which there is general consensus. However, we have only to look to the history of this country in the last 160 years or so, to realise that really important values can and do change. For example, our value system (and the laws that go with them) have altered so that we do not deport children (or adults) for stealing; divorced mothers are not automatically deprived of access to their own children; we do not oblige women to resign from work if they marry; do not bar people from public office because they are not Anglicans or men. Values, attitudes and the law have changed with respect to the mentally ill and physically disabled, to men's and women's roles at work and in the family, to sexuality; and require that people of colour be treated with respect. But there are more immediate and local examples of different interpretations of values. For instance, in one school, children spend a designated hour of each week in church; in another they spend an hour at the library. In one family it might be inconceivable to disregard one's parents' and in-laws' views; in another the young family lives its own way, with reference to a peer group rather than 'original roots'. This reflects not so much relativism as pluralism – with different values operating alongside each other, reflecting both the speed of change and the increasing complexity of society.

In this complex situation, how does one decide between competing values? Midgley (1997) warns us that morality is contiguous with the rest of our social lives, as members of communities: it is not just a matter of individual values. People's morality is based on choices and seeing reasons for doing things, not just on fear of punishment. If you don't respect or accept the values of the people trying to persuade you or threatening to punish you, there is little chance that you will change your mind. Midgley (1991) says that it is not helpful to look for certainty based on 'a single foundation stone of truth', but that we require suitable answers for real questions and need to make our judgements about what is right and good with relation to the *consequences* of any decision. In deciding whether or not something is right and good, we should always be rational, take responsibility (be accountable), accept the logic of our own decisions and be prepared to change them in the light of new evidence.

'Human rights' offers an umbrella for considering our values with respect to practices at home and abroad. Guided by principles of human rights, one feels confident in condemning torture, the recruitment of young children into armed conflict or sexual exploitation. However, the principle of human rights will not necessarily tell us what to do in situations where the human rights of individuals or groups are in conflict, or when disputes about incompatible values arise. Such dilemmas are inevitable in a plural society. In other words, it is not always possible to 'read off' the solution, simply by calling on human rights.

To help readers sort out their own position and help design and handle debates with children about justice, rights and responsibilities in a democracy, here are some approaches drawn from political philosophy.

a. *Deontologists* – believe that there are certain moral rules, typically coming from religion, and that one has a duty to obey and live by these. You will recognise this as moral absolutism.

b. *Utilitarians* – are pragmatic about justice and rights in society. The test of a moral belief and action lies in its consequences and the guiding principle of utilitarianism is 'the greatest good for the greatest number', which underpins much of our political process. Deontologists might say you should not execute criminals because it is always wrong to kill another human being; utilitarians would say the test of capital punishment is whether criminals were deterred. However, utilitarianism does not make way uncritically for unjust majority rule. The great nineteenth-century utilitarian John Stuart Mill was *against* slavery in the Southern States of America, and *for* votes for women in Britain, at a time when neither would have won a majority in their respective countries if there had been a referendum. The justification he gave was that abolition of slavery and votes for women would actually both be better for society than the current situation, though not everyone could see this.

Rule utilitarians decide on a rule which they intend to benefit the majority and then stick to it.

Act utilitarians consider the consequences of individual actions rather than following a pre-ordained rule.

The soaps children watch on television often provide scenarios in which to explore such ideas. A fascinating example of the clash between these two versions of utilitarianism arose in an episode of ER in early 2001. Dr. Weaver wanted to (and did) report illegal Guatemalan workers because she knew this was against the law. Dr. Kovaks was concerned that reporting them would lead to an awful catastrophe in their workplace (which is what happened in the story).

c. *Rawls and the rules for a just multicultural society*
Even if we are entirely in favour of human rights as a principle of justice, this does not necessarily help us decide what to do in situations of conflict. John Rawls is among the giants of political philo-

sophy of the twentieth century, whose ideas could help children debate issues of human rights and justice.

His first principle is that in a democratic community we must all agree to raise, argue and debate issues of justice in a way which does not assume in advance that one's own values and principles are superior. In other words, one must ensure that everyone can participate on an equal footing. Moral questions which are best addressed in private, such as religious questions, should be kept separate from questions about justice. This will go some way to allowing everyone to participate as equals in public debates.

Secondly, it is essential that everyone agrees on basic principles of justice which apply to everyone, even if the rationalisations come from different political or religious creeds.

John Rawls put justice, fairness, rights and duties of responsible citizens at the heart of his discussion about a just society. 'Rights' theorists, as they are called, following his lead, believe in inalienable human rights. The difficulty in practice is that my 'rights' may clash with your 'rights'. So I may claim a right to play my music loudly, while you claim the right to peace and quiet. This scenario, based on different cultural norms, can lead to conflict in a community, as Vince Hines (1998) has pointed out. At its simplest, you can resolve the conflict by agreeing that no one person's rights should transgress another person's rights, but even this doesn't always provide a ready-made answer to conflict.

Justice and the 'veil of ignorance'

Rawls offers us a procedure to decide what is fair *whoever we are*, using what he calls 'the veil of ignorance'. This is a fascinating idea, which can easily be turned into a game in the classroom. The idea is that you have to decide on a course of action without knowing in advance who you are in the scenario. This prevents your acting on the basis of self-interest. So in the loud music scenario above, you have to put your real identity and preferences on hold and decide what is fair, without knowing whether you are the person who enjoys heavy metal at full volume or the person next door with a splitting headache and a sick child. When the 'veil of ignorance' is lifted, you should be happy with the outcome whoever you are.

Suppose the group is considering housework, or access to resources. They decide that women should be in charge of all the housework, and men in charge of earning the daily bread, or that Y6 should have first go on the computers, because they are the oldest and all younger children should wait their turn. The test of justice and fairness is how they feel about this decision when they discover whether they are a female or a male or in Y2 and not Y6 (decided by cards handed out randomly).

The theory does not prevent you from privileging some groups and discriminating in a positive way, eg on behalf of disabled children, on the basis of 'to each according to their needs'. In real life, there are always situations where a group or individual may have to go without something and the game can be used to help children consider positive action. For example, there may be only five places on a course, or limited tickets to a special event. You could pull names out of a hat, but you might decide instead that you wanted specific people to benefit. Children would need to understand about the 'veil of ignorance' as they made their decision about who should benefit. The most poignant examples of this principle in action are life and death decisions, eg about allocation of donor organs. Depending on the age of the children, you may want to have them debate such real life dilemmas, guided by the 'veil of ignorance' principle.

d. Care, compassion and responsibility – feminist critiques of the Rawlsian justice/fairness/rights/duties discourse

A number of feminist philosophers have pointed out that Rawls' views on justice and rights are all very well, but that few people make decisions in this way. For example, the relationships between parents and their children or loving partners are based not so much on rights and obligations as on care, trust and love. Feminist moral philosophers would be unimpressed with rule utilitarianism which pronounces that 'it's wrong to steal', or 'it's wrong to fight' in every situation. Instead, they have developed the ideas of act utilitarianism arguing that one needs to consider the actual relationships between the people involved, and make decisions that are concerned with consequences but based on genuine care and empathy. So it might be right to fight to defend one's child who is in danger of being hurt; it might be justified to steal a drug if it were the only way to keep a loved person alive. Tolerance of ambiguity then becomes an indication of higher order morality, not of moral inferiority. The feminist philosopher Nell Noddings (1984) suggests that morality is not just about rational thinking but also the willingness to step out of our own shoes and consider someone else's point of view, plus a commitment to protect or enhance the welfare of other people.

Such considerations, initially introduced by feminists but increasingly shared by male philosophers, have a clear connection to the issues in this book. Bonnett, for example, points out that thinking about justice and fairness – moral thinking, if you like – always concerns feelings and the ability to empathise with others. Carol Gilligan, who has done much research with children, adolescents and adults about moral thinking, initially suggested that characteristics of care, compassion and responsibility were typically female (Gilligan, 1982). However, recent research has shown that rights and care are not gender-specific discourses – girls and boys, men and women all draw on these ideas. The boys in this book were as likely to reflect the morality of care and compassion as girls were to talk about rights. For myself, I have found that a combination of the philosophical positions helps decision-making in different contexts.

Even decisions about strangers are imbued with values and there is no logical reason to exclude care, compassion and concern for others when trying to resolve conflict in a fair and just manner. A world in which we are only prepared to be involved with people elsewhere because it is in our interests or because we are related offers a bleak, desolate kind of morality. With children it is sensible to start with the classroom and playground and then move into a wider community of people whom one does not know personally, moving from the local into the wider world. Unfortunately, there is little evidence at present that primary teachers are giving children opportunities to think about issues in a wider context than their school. History, geography and literature are all possible vehicles for such work and so is religious education, particularly through the second attainment target, 'learning from religion', which focuses on the common values of compassion, charity and care in the major religions (as opposed to AT1, 'learning about religions').

A good person and a good citizen?

How far does personal morality overlap with public morality and values? The paragraphs above suggest continuities and so does the structure of the PSHE/Ct guidance for KS1 and 2. Moving beyond individual instances that children may bring to the classroom, feminist thinking back in the 1970s challenged us to consider how far 'the personal is political', pointing out that domestic violence and child abuse were the private face of injustice. In recent years the behaviour of individuals in the privacy of their homes has become a matter of public concern where it transgresses human rights. Agents of the state may intervene if a child is battered or exploited; a woman who is abused has recourse to the law. It was not always so, and there is still some way to go in ensuring human rights for all people, children too, within our own state, let alone across the world. However, an acknowledgement of these continuities, and awareness of how power used oppressively in personal situations can transgress human rights, helps sort out what our attitudes might be and how and why we might decide to intervene.

Education as transformation – empowerment

This last section takes on a central plank of the maximalist agenda of citizenship, namely that education should equip children to transform their society and not just be a means to retain the status quo. Views about 'an ideal citizen' and how democracy works have determined the nature of citizenship education. The current situation is that democratic processes and representation are assumed to work. If they do not, public apathy or inappropriate direct action is blamed. There is no acknowledgement that the state itself might favour one group over another, which may then feel disenfranchised and disempowered within the democracy. The obvious discrepancies relate to racism, sexism and disability. Because the inequalities within society are not acknowledged, it is possible to believe that consensus can be negotiated to everyone's satisfaction without addressing the distribution and exercise of power.

Paolo Freire (quoted by Torres, 1998) pointed out that it was unrealistic to expect any society to put in place an educational system which might undermine its own power. On the other hand, if a society takes a dynamic view which recognises the necessity for growth, change and transformation in the light of current and future developments, then a system which educates children to critique existing systems is seen to be in the society's interests. Education and teachers then become part of the process through which children are politicised, not so much for conformity and compliance but to participate in a public debate about possibilities for transformation. The difficulty is, as Freire himself realised, that just as a compliant, conformist education for citizenship is manipulative, an emancipatory education may be guilty of indoctrination. The key seems to be to equip children to think for themselves, to have the means to critique through weighing evidence, and the emotional and intellectual ability to conduct rational argument. Within this model, the emphasis on self-esteem, understanding and tolerance makes good sense, since personal characteristics of this kind are more likely to support the abilities to discuss difficult issues rationally than poor self-esteem, envy and intolerance.

Freire said that enlisting children in one or another specifically political cause is not the task of the teacher but that education can support emancipation through helping children understand the social structures. This links directly with some of the ways in which inequalities in our society have been analysed in recent reports such as the Inquiry into the death of Stephen Lawrence (Macpherson, 1999), and the Parekh Report. These reports emphasise structural and institutional racism, the antithesis of personalised analyses that blame antisocial 'rotten apples' in a basically sound system. As we saw in Chapter 3, racism is central to the experience of children in inner-city schools, often on a daily basis, and we do them no favours by individualising racism and denying children the intellectual tools to combat it.

In recent years in Britain, the Development Education movement has challenged teachers to think about the ways in which a sound and healthy democracy requires people to critique their own society and, imagine alternative scenarios and solutions. Children's understanding of their society and, ultimately, their ability to envision something better is supported, not undermined, by helping them understand the institutionalised structures which discriminate against minority groups, refugees and asylum seekers, women, people with disabilities, gays and lesbians.

The subject matter of the next chapter is economics – national and global. Economics, despite its bad press in some quarters, is imbued with values, consequently readers will find links and continuities with this chapter. I continue to explore ideas, values and concepts which children need in order to make sense of the society they live in and to become educated citizens empowered to envision and promote a better future for themselves.

7

The responsible citizen: tools for thinking

A radical curriculum: including economics in political literacy

What should children know and understand about economics? What part does it play in political literacy and active citizenship in the twenty-first century, to take them beyond some of the misunderstandings and confusions which surfaced in the stories they volunteered, discussed in Chapter 5.

The National Curriculum refers twice to economic understanding, first in the Values, Aims and Purposes Statement, which looks to the future and 'prepar(ing) pupils for the next steps in their education, training and employment and equip(ping) them to make informed choices ... including employment' (p. 12). The KS 2 guidance for PSHE/Ct suggests pupils should know about the range of jobs in society, understand how they can develop skills to make their own contribution, learn to look after their money and realise that future wants and needs may be met through saving (1e and f); 2j requires that children learn 'that resources can be allocated in different ways, and these economic choices affect individuals, communities and the sustainability of the environment' (p.139).

Genuine preparation for the choices and understanding implied by the statements above requires access to ideas which will not be found in the traditional primary curriculum, for example:

- what should responsible 'consuming citizens' in the local and national sphere know and understand about the wider effects of their choices?

- what should a citizen of the 'North' understand about economic interdependence with the lives of poorer people in the 'South' (the global dimensions of citizenship)?
- how can we make sense of choices made on our behalf by public bodies like the council and government and, in some cases, charities?

Some may say 'why not wait till KS 3?' The justification is the same as for introducing anything else into the primary years: the notion of the spiral curriculum which builds appropriate foundations, working from what children already know something about – even if such understanding is confused and partial.

Some economic concepts are so fundamental to a genuine citizenship curriculum that one should be enquiring why they have been marginalised, rather than justifying their inclusion. The concepts and ideologies underpinning welfare economics and social policy are the stuff of election programmes, regeneration policies, community interventions. When plans are made to improve the environment or the transport system or health provision, or anything else that affects the quality of life in the community, it is impossible to say anything sensible about processes and outcomes without referring to economic concepts. Sadly, there are no free lunches: work on change and sustainability which does not start with the concepts of limited resources and unavoidable choices is pointless and irresponsible. Work about resource allocation requires the appropriate conceptual tools for the job, otherwise it's wasting everyone's time.

There is a missing link in the current agenda for citizenship. Economics, as well as political ideology, determines how the community and the country are governed in practice. Moreover, active global citizenship is largely a matter of making sense of the economic inter-relationships between the developed and the developing world (sometimes called 'North and South' though geographically these labels aren't always accurate).

All political decision-making in a democracy is based on two central tenets, *both* of which should be the subject of debate and education within the school system:

- the value systems underpinning the nature of the society we want
- the practical methods – the reality – of implementing those values through projects/programmes which must be resourced through the allocation of funds.

Both are necessary, and neither is sufficient on its own.

The current practice is to get started on the first in the primary school and to neglect the second, probably on the grounds that the subject is too hard, too dry, too specialised. But this need not be true. The basic ideas in economics education are no harder than the (compulsory) maths we teach, and can be contextualised in practical classroom debate.

I will not attempt to offer a crash course in economics here but will limit myself to some of basic ideas about how decisions are made within a welfare state, and about global connections.

Citizens as responsible consumers

The starting point for much primary education in economics is based on personal choices about spending, captured by the aphorism 'you can't have your cake and eat it'. Suppose you have 10p to spend, and can choose between a wiggle and a woggle, each costing 10p. You can't have both. The choice you are forced into is called 'opportunity cost'. Opportunity cost is important because it emphasises that in any choice, you will think about the respective benefits. Your judgement about the benefits will be based on your values. For the wiggle/woggle example, opportunity cost may reflect values (benefits) to do with your own health (the woggle may be better for your teeth) but as far as citizenship education goes, this is all rather limited. Children need to move from the personal into the public sphere and explore the wider ramifications of consumer choices. They need to consider firstly, the public costs and benefits within their own community or country and, secondly, the costs and benefits to communities far away. I will start with the first idea, using examples which are transferable into primary classroom work.

The difference between private costs and benefits and public (social) costs and benefits

Options are seldom clear-cut, in either personal or public choices. It is part of children's developing understanding to be able to consider the network of consequences as well as the reasons for consumer choices, and to be able to think about values for other people who will be affected. As I argued in Chapter 6, considering values and consequences of choices should be part of thinking about fair allocation of resources.

Scenario 1: Salim Ali's dad takes him to school each morning in the car. It takes him out of his way, but it means that Mrs Ali doesn't have to get baby Jasmeen up and ready first thing (since she can't leave her at home) and Salim has a comfortable ride in the back seat. Those are the *benefits* to Salim and his family. The *private costs* for Salim's family are the petrol, wear and tear on the car, wear and tear on Mr Ali's nerves from the traffic, finding and paying for a parking space when he gets to work. However, let's say the Ali family feels the benefits outweigh the costs – which is why they go ahead with this on a daily basis.

The *public benefits* of the Ali's consumer choice are few. Jasmeen's asthma might be worse if she is taken out in the morning, so she would have to go to the doctor – which the NHS pays for – so perhaps we're saving something there. The council gets some revenue from the meter where Mr Ali parks near his work.

The *public costs* are considerable: Mr Ali's car is one more clogging up the roads at 8.45 am, adding to pollution, wear and tear on the roads and possibilities of accidents at rush hour. There is also a relationship between car pollution and childhood asthma – the NHS budget again. Mr Ali parks his car near his work, a busy commercial area which is metered to control the car inflow, and the council has to supervise and service this and operate a tow-away system and a car pound.

While you can probably put a monetary value on the personal costs and even the public costs (though it's harder) it is more difficult to put a monetary value against the benefits. We'll come back to that.

Scenario 2: Chantal Williams' mum has been told that it is healthier to cut back on meat and eat more vegetables. She'll need to persuade her family (maybe get into fierce arguments), may have to spend more time preparing vegetables and so on – these will be costs. However, she is convinced that for all their health, the benefits outweigh the costs.

But what about the *social* costs and benefits of her decision? On its own, just like Mr Ali's car journey, it hardly counts. But if a great many people start changing from meat to vegetables there is a knock-on effect: first there will be a rush on vegetables – and a shortage – so that market traders realise they can charge more. But that would be short term, because pretty soon farmers would get their act together to produce more and prices would stabilise again. Perhaps farmers in Norfolk would start developing their farming methods and in due course some of them would get richer from the improved market for their produce. And what about the butcher shops and the meat farmers: people will no longer want their produce, their profits are hit – they will have to lay off workers, they may go bust. The butcher may be able to find a job somewhere else, though without using his existing skills. The meat farmers can't just turn their grazing land into vegetable farms. A large area of the country – Wales or Cumbria – could be affected.

On the one hand, this is still a matter of private costs and benefits – Norfolk vegetable farmers and Welsh or Cumbrian sheep farmers considered as individuals whose businesses boom and bust with changing patterns of consumption. But if the sheep farmers' problems increase, the government will become involved: perhaps to subsidise them, perhaps to help them convert to something that will sell. The government may not really want everyone to return to large-scale meat eating, because health improves with more vegetables in the diet and this reduces NHS expenditure. Vegetables are cheaper, which is good for poorer people, so there are benefits there. This example illustrates how hard it can be to calculate the 'value' of the benefits in terms of money.

The point is that the Williams' family's original decision to substitute vegetables for some meat may be absolutely right on health grounds but that one family's decision is usually part of something much larger, whether 'managed' by advertising or government, or part of changing patterns of consumption. It may not be necessary or appropriate for primary children's discussion to go any further than unpicking the strands of the argument, so that they can appreciate how personal and public decisions interact.

The global connections

We can extrapolate this example to consider consumption of goods made or grown abroad and see how our actions and choices affect people far away. Oxfam has produced useful material which shows that the producers get a fractional amount of the price we pay at our end, because so much goes to intermediaries, transport costs, profits to the retailer and so on. These scenarios, usually in the form of games, are helpful for children taking other perspectives and understanding inter-relationships. But they tend to avoid two problems. The first concerns whether and how much more consumers are prepared to spend so that the original producer (farmer) gets a fairer wage. (I come back to issues about exploitation of workers later in this chapter.) The second problem is more complex and may be health-based, like the one about meat-eating: if there is a move away from coffee (tobacco, sugar, opium) in the West, say on health grounds, not only the wholesalers, importers and retailers but, maybe worst of all, the farmers in eg. Colombia, Kenya, Jamaica will be affected – and they will have nothing to fall back on. What should happen now? Who should be helping the poor farmers in the producing countries?

Put like this, the dilemmas of global responsibility become apparent. Children need time to construct diagrams which show the connections, and time to unravel the complexities so that they don't fall into knee-jerk reactions. It's not simple but it may ultimately be the most honest and productive way to consider improvements for poorer people in the world through 'joined-up thinking' which reflects some of the real issues that have to be thrashed out. I return to global issues towards the end of this chapter but now move back to national ones.

Public choices about how citizens' money is spent

Interpreted broadly, political literacy would acknowledge the centrality of economics in the agenda of any political party, whether at election time or mid-term. Some children raised these concerns themselves, without prompting, but the traditional agenda of electioneering can provide a list of issues that children might debate. The following edited summary comes from the election manifestos of 2001.

1. *Health* – increases in community care, particularly for the elderly
2. *Crime* – reductions in vehicle crime, burglary, robbery, fear of crime and re-offending; cases brought to justice increase
3. *Asylum* – reduction in decision period for asylum applicants
4. *Education* – improved SATs results at Key Stages 2 and 3, GCSE and adult literacy; extra places for childcare; reduction in truancy
5. *Children and Poverty* – reduction of pregnant mothers who smoke; establishment of national child-minders register
6. *Welfare* – numbers of children living in low income households to fall; reform of child support scheme; reform of pension schemes including for people on low incomes, carers, disabled people; target for majority of claimants to have benefits paid into bank accounts; reduction in fraud and error in income support and job seekers' allowances; target for people leaving care to be better off and more skilled; adoption figures to increase; cost of acute care to fall
7. *Jobs and the economy* – fall in unemployment, particularly in disadvantaged areas; improved employment rates for people with disabilities, lone parents, ethnic minorities, over-50s
8. *Environment and Transport* – improvements in air quality; improved recycling, energy efficiency; reduction in numbers living in sub-standard housing; new target for bringing abandoned houses back into use; increase in new housing; reduction in rail and road congestion; increased use of buses; opening up public

access to countryside; cut in numbers killed in fire and traffic deaths; reduce days lost through work-related ill-health or injury

9. *Culture* – increase children's visits to museums and galleries and the numbers of people experiencing arts
10. *Industry* – increased productivity; improve economic performance in regions; reduce prices for gas and electricity
11. *Drugs* – reduction in numbers using Class A drugs, reduction in availability of Class A drugs and offending by Class A drug users; increased participation in treatment
12. *Criminal Justice* – reduce time between charge and sentence/ dismissal, particularly for young offenders
13. *Food* – reduce food-borne illness (eg salmonella, BSE)
14. *International Development* – increase proportion of assistance going to poorest countries
15. *Defence* – meet full staffing requirements for RAF, navy and army; increase capacity and readiness
16. *Foreign affairs* – new target for signing comprehensive test ban treaty; global regulation of oceans and commitment to combat climate change; international understanding on drugs and crime

Though it would be unreasonable to expect KS 2 children to understand and be able to work with the sophisticated economics that underpins these programmes or to engage with all the areas, some are within their consideration.

How does government (or councils) intervene in our lives?

As part of political literacy, children could consider responsibility and accountability in certain areas of political life, for instance:

- *funding and managing major public services* like the army and navy, the police and courts, the Health Service, education, roads. Railways, coal, gas, steel and electricity used to be managed by the British Government when they were nationalised industries, but the situation has changed. Governments are prepared to subsidise some areas which private firms would not undertake without profits, in the interests of the general economy and welfare of the people.

- *transferring money from one set of people to others*, through the taxation system, via social security benefits and unemployment benefits – ie making the Welfare State work.

There are different theories about how best to do these things, though there are not huge differences in the approaches taken by middle-of-the-road governments from either political party. Right-wing Conservative governments believe in letting the free market determine the economy, leaving as much as possible in the hands of private industries and individuals, believing that their concern to maximise profits will lead to greater efficiency. Similarly, they hold that Government should not provide too much in 'transfer payments' because it is better for people to get their money through working and producing something than through hand-outs. Socialist governments tend to believe that the economy is far too complex to be left completely to itself and that it needs to be regulated through an overall plan even if aspects are funded through the private sector. Secondly, that there are some projects which are socially advisable but not necessarily profitable and, unless government takes responsibility, the quality of life for some will suffer. Thirdly, in modern society there are many people who may fall through the net, through no fault of their own and that governments should take responsibility to look after them through the welfare system.

In the last decade of the twentieth century we seemed at times to be returning to Victorian ideas about *the role of charity* in acting as a safety net for the poorest but the non-governmental organisations of today are very different from the charities of the nineteenth century and the change of name itself signals an important difference. As organisations like Shelter or Save the Children gain more support from individuals, so their power with respect to government itself grows. These NGOs now have a part in policy-making; their reports about conditions are taken seriously by government; they receive large grants or subsidies and some of their projects may well be funded by government. There is a message here for children about grassroots participation, individual empowerment and democracy.

The power of NGOs to influence change should affect how schools interpret the guidance to 'recognise the role of voluntary, community and pressure groups'. Children might consider the size, power and particular ethical position of the big NGOs with respect to poverty, discussed later in this chapter. Visiting old people's homes, sponsoring a child or establishing email links with a school in India may address empathy, but such activities can leave children with simplistic, limited understandings of how change can be effected in an unequal world.

Some concepts from economics to enable understanding of these ideas

1. Economics is about how to manage resources in conditions of scarcity, when there is not enough to have everything you might want (otherwise there is no problem of choice or management). This goes for both personal budgeting and macroeconomics.

2. Though there are some overlapping concepts, Governments and local authorities are *not* like families or businesses, because the latter try to balance their budget or make profits, and these are not Government's main concerns.

3. Governments and councils take responsibility for some aspects of life which are not profit-making but which are considered to have social value and whose benefits are spread about (for example all the different areas of social life that education benefits).

4. Any programme has to be paid for – education, transport, health care, welfare or the police service – and there are always competing demands and a ceiling on funds available to the Government or Local Authority. So opportunity costs must be part of any debate about what to do.

5. To understand why there are never enough funds to do absolutely everything that would be 'a good thing', children need to realise that the money comes either from taxes – direct and indirect – or raising loans (borrowing).

Taxes: when a government lowers income tax, it usually finds ways to replenish the coffers through indirect taxes like VAT on goods and services, the lottery, and additional taxes on petrol, cigarettes, alcohol. The conventional wisdom is that high direct taxes/low indirect taxes hit the rich more than the poor and that low direct taxes/high indirect taxes hit the poor, who don't come into the higher tax brackets anyway. This seems an important point for children to grasp, particularly those coming from poorer socio-economic backgrounds who will be the very ones paying more indirect taxes relative to their whole budget. But they might also need to realise that lowering income tax is not just partisan behaviour to the wealthy, but that it has to do with stimulating the economy as a whole and that, theoretically, people can choose not to buy the things that are indirectly taxed as long as these are not essential.

There is a limit to the amount that can be raised through taxes. If you set income tax too high, hoping to get huge revenue, people won't be left with enough to spend on the rest of their needs, and that will hit the economy too (through demand going down). And anyway, you'll probably get voted out at the next election! If indirect taxes go too high, people will stop buying the goods or services, so that will be self-defeating.

Children should be able to grasp these ideas about the limits on government or council revenue which can be raised from tax, especially if they are set up as flow diagrams, or children are asked to design 'election posters' or take sides in a mock debate.

Raising loans: Governments can carry loans for years without repaying them. Keynesian theory suggests that it is a good thing for a government to invest in major public works to provide jobs and income to people, even if it needs to do so through loans. Governments can subsidise social projects which are not breaking even, through loans. But they can't just keep on raising loans if they do not have a sufficiently strong economy for the lenders to believe their money is 'safe'. This links to the state of the internal economy and also its international position. These are probably not ideas primary children can take very far, except that they might consider the situation for countries in the developing world which may have difficulty raising or repaying loans because their economies are weak and who are forced to go along with the policies and requirements of stronger, wealthier countries (the 'North') who finance the loans.

Costs, benefits and value systems

In the section about how personal choices had knock-on effects in the public sphere, I introduced the ideas of costs, benefits and putting values on the benefits. Now I develop the arguments about how 'values' link with public costs and benefits.

Making decisions about what to do in the public sector

Faced with a decision about funding a project, all the following ideas need to be considered:

- the *values* you hold (eg police on the street are 'a good thing' to discourage crime; nurseries for three year olds are a good thing rather than expecting parents to take sole responsibility)
- the *cost* of your programme (putting two police on duty on every market day and available at all times in the estates; building, staffing and running the nurseries)
- *the hoped-for benefits* of the programme (crime goes down, people feel safer; children's academic and social record later shows improvements; parents able to go to work)
- the *probability of success* (a hard one, but very important). Crime really does have to go down, people do have to feel safer or the whole thing is a waste of time and money. The three-year olds do have to show improvements in various criteria and their parents do have to get jobs
- *opportunity cost – what you will have to give up* in order to have more police on the beat or fund the nurseries (eg station officers on duty answering calls; funding the University of the Third Age).

If you don't want to give up the station officers or the University of the Third Age, then you have to find extra money for your extended programmes. Other programmes are also competing for public money; values and the comparative costs and benefits will determine the ultimate decision.

Here is another example, worked through in a school setting. Should you spend funds on a concept keyboard or on new outdoor equipment for the Early Years Base? You have to consider:

- your *values* – the concept keyboard compared with the outdoor equipment
- the *cost* of the two projects – buying the computer, installing it, service contract, training nursery staff; buying and installing the play equipment
- the *hoped-for benefits* of the programme – needs of various nursery children get met, though some will benefit more than others, according to the project
- the *probability of success* – an evaluation will provide evidence that the identified nursery children benefit measurably
- the *opportunity cost* – you can't have both so you must choose

Let's suppose there are currently only three children in the nursery who would benefit from the concept keyboard, but that 35 children would benefit from the outdoor equipment (let's say they cost the same). Do you want to privilege the larger number of children or support the smaller number with special needs? This discussion would draw on concepts that were discussed in the previous chapter: 'the veil of ignorance', privileging special needs and feminist ideas about care and concern for others.

Separating out the costs and benefits and the values we place on them

One can think about the costs and benefits of some choice without making value judgements. Conflicts between political parties or pressure groups usually arise not because they claim that the costs and benefits will differ, but because they value the potential benefits differently. However, you can only have a sensible, realistic discussion about what you should do if you are prepared to analyse costs and benefits as well as values.

Children can be reminded that pressure groups are by definition self-interested and will argue loudly and persuasively for the benefits and values of their preferred programme. The petroleum industry will manipulate our ideas about the value of using private vehicles; dog lovers will argue about the value to mental health and security of dog ownership. This may be part of the way we develop a 'value'. In the end, we have to choose!

There's one more consideration which we should introduce, namely *probability*. It would be downright irresponsible to spend large amounts on an education programme against say, smoking, if there was absolutely no evidence that it worked. This came up recently: it seems that the huge and expensive national programme to persuade teenagers not to smoke was having virtually no effect. So even though it is 'a good thing', it has little benefit because it's not working.

This might all seem long-winded and, at any event, beyond the capacities of primary children. But doesn't this relate to our own education? Few of us have been taught to consider these matters in such detail. Yet it is in the interests of democracy that people start to get to grips with these ideas. If it's all set out logically, using Carroll diagrams or spider charts, flow charts or mental maps, children can start to appreciate the ramifications of sorting out some problem. Here's a start:

The grid opposite sets out some of the areas of life, all familiar to children, along with some of the social costs and social benefits. You and your pupils may disagree with me, in which case you should substitute your own ideas.

Next, put a value on both benefits and costs, that is indicate how much you care about either. If you value the social benefits more than the social costs, then you should keep/expand the programme. If not, you should consider an alternative.

Where can the funding come from?

There has been little attempt to help children understand the funding of programmes in a mixed economy with a welfare ethic, or the relationship between taxation, subsidies, charities and conventional business costs. The result can be that children think that anything in

Area of social activity	Social costs	Social benefits
Using private cars and lorries	roads get worn down; air becomes polluted; traffic congestion slows people down; accidents increase	goods transported quickly and efficiently to your door; privacy during journeys; motor industry kept buoyant
Packaging	pollution; getting rid of waste; recycling	good for advertising; keeps things clean/hygienic/in good shape; good for brand name maintenance
Tobacco smoking	air pollution; health related costs with wide ramifications including to babies and children of parents who smoke	private, personal choices of many people maintained; we shouldn't live in a 'nanny state'; raises revenue for health service; keeps some people in jobs
Mobile phones	noise pollution; possible radiation danger for people near the masts; vehicle accidents	quick, efficient communication; has brought costs of phone calls down

the public sphere is possible if you want it enough, or that cake stalls or 'going to the bank' will provide the funding.

Much of what happens in primary economics education (if it happens at all) is about little private enterprises and the need to break even, make profits and run a business which supplies some product at a price people are prepared to pay. Thus, children set up little enterprises in school and find out through personal experience how to get a loan from the bank, attract custom through advertising, price their product to meet the demand and make a profit. This is helpful experience which relates to much economic life but as far as public spending goes it is limited. It's rather as if children are being prepared for a self-financing world of private schools, private hospitals, private housing estates, private transport schemes.

The issue about who should fund programmes for development and improvement warrants discussion in its own right. Private firms don't provide services which are unprofitable or they go out of business: if a council decides to rely on private buses to serve an area late at night and it's not profitable, there are unlikely to be any buses. On the other hand, the council may decide there's an important social value in the late night buses and run them at a loss, subsidising the expense from taxes collected elsewhere.

Should charities take the main roles, for example in developing a playground space near their school or dealing with the homeless, or should the responsibility lie with the council or private individuals or their own families, through the indirect taxation of the lottery fund? There are arguments for and against all these sources. In the end it is 'us', ordinary people, who support charities, buy lottery tickets and pay taxes. We have some choice in the first two but not in the last.

Private firms can also be persuaded to fund public projects. Waitrose, Tescos and Sainsburys have all followed this route. Arsenal Football Club has a stake in local developments near its grounds. Such involvement is good for their image and increases their status and credibility in the local area. Large firms have profits which can be invested in such schemes and they are rewarded through the government taxation system for such investments. They have profits because we, the customers, buy their goods in the first place. But there can be ethical dilemmas, as when Nike funded an education programme in America and parents realised their children were benefiting at the expense of children in Vietnam who worked in Nike factories for appallingly low wages (Klein, 2001:368)

Lastly, the Government or Council might take responsibility for programmes. They may be the only organisations prepared to undertake something which is seen as socially beneficial but which is costly and requires subsidising. For example, they may undertake to demolish an estate that has proved problematic environmentally and socially, and fund rebuilding. These funds have to come from taxation, whether direct or indirect. This includes money for the various regeneration schemes funded by the European Union – which also comes ultimately from taxpayers but goes wider than England.

Who should pay for the social costs of modern urban life?

After we have helped children think about the ways in which costs and benefits have to be considered and valued, we might get them to consider who should pay the social costs incurred by various actions. Currently, it isn't the people who create the social cost (the pollution, the noise, the mess in the streets) who pay for it. In the case of car/ lorry use, should the government put an extra tax on petrol and diesel, so as to pay for the expenses and to deter people from using their vehicles? A recent lorry strike showed what can happen: a pressure group was sufficiently powerful to challenge government action. But there is also the problem that increased costs for transport get passed on to us, the consumers. So in the end, it is likely that ordinary people pay.

Should the government manage pollution through making laws about engine design, even if congestion and accidents aren't affected? Shall it be parking metres and parking fines, pedestrianised areas preventing car drivers coming into the inner areas? The latter will entail provision of better public transport – and will that come out of council taxes? Or what about lower bus fares, that is, subsidising public transport. How should this be paid for – out of taxes perhaps, using the argument that the social benefits are high enough to justify this?

Becoming a global citizen

Today's world is one of unprecedented global change, with many new challenges to the notion of citizenship. Unless children are introduced to the new concepts and the new realities, their participation in the real issues of world democracy and human rights will be severely limited.

The connection between human rights and poverty

Rich-poor relationships are complex and it is forgivable to feel powerless in the face of the forces involved. Understanding the centrality of human rights issues in the rich/poor global agenda can help teachers clarify their own approaches to the work they offer children. A recent United Nations Development Report (UNDP, 2000) stated that *the economic and social situation of the poorest people in any country relates directly to its human rights record.* Poverty is not just about having insufficient money or nice clothes or food, as the children in this book defined it. Human rights are defined in terms of clean water, decent health care, education, housing and work, and because these amenities are seldom available to those living in poverty, they are deemed to be suffering human rights abuse. The poor are exploited economically and, typically, are not in a position to make their voices heard. To be a global citizen and not only concerned about one's own backyard involves drawing on the Rawlsian ideas discussed in Chapter 6, and exercising care, compassion and empathy. To imagine that it might be *you* in a particular situation, and consider what you would want to happen, can be the powerful starting point for global concern. Children can understand the links between their own lives and the lives of others in the world through coming to terms with the issues set out below.

What does Globalisation mean?

Globalisation dates from the break-up of the Soviet block after the Berlin Wall came down and China entered the world of market economies. Many countries which had been protectionist opened up their borders to trade, formalised in 1994 when the World Trade

Organisation was set up to regulate global trade. The WTO is currently the target of considerable protest, since the poorer, less developed nations consider that the terms of trade benefit the wealthy nations and are loaded against them. The violent forms of protest adopted recently would be worth discussing in class. The clash in values between violent and peaceful protest has a long history. In the Edwardian period suffragettes used arson and smashed windows, while suffragists confined themselves to speeches and marches. Children might consider peaceful protests such as the Hunger Marches of the 1930s, Gandhi's Civil Disobedience campaign, the Civil Rights demonstrations of the 1960s in the USA or the women's camps at Greenham Common in the 1980s.

Globalisation involves increasing interactions of all kinds across national boundaries and also, paradoxically, increasing fragmentation and inequality in some areas. Increased interactions are in the form of greater and faster exports between countries, much more foreign investment, more foreign travel, more communication through the net and telephone, more migration between countries and through the operations of multinationals.

Though *foreign investment and exports* have increased and speeded up, this is not evenly spread – countries like China, Mexico and Brazil have benefited far more than Pakistan, Peru or Colombia. The top 20% of people in the richest countries enjoy the benefits of the increases; the bottom 20% have scarcely been affected. This means that many developing countries have become further marginalised. This is one example of how globalisation fragments rather than integrates.

Globalisation of *communication technologies* has meant there's more of it, it's quicker and also much cheaper, transforming the nature of 'network societies'. The UNDP Report claims that 'national borders are breaking down, not only for trade, capital and information but also for ideas, norms, cultures and values.' (2000:29)

The ways in which attitudes to people from developing countries interlock with human rights and globalisation are starkly illustrated by *migration* in this century. We are a long way from the nineteenth century, when Irish, Germans, Scandinavians and Jews set out from Europe for a new life across the oceans.

Some migration in the twenty first century is official, particularly for skilled workers who are welcomed, but a great deal is unofficial, particularly for unskilled workers seeking a livelihood, called economic migrants, who tend to come from the poorest countries of the world. The money they send back home is a major source of foreign exchange in some countries, particularly India, Mexico and Turkey, so the host country helps poorer people in developing countries in this way. But migration of unskilled workers without papers has led to discrimination and denial of human rights, since they may be forced to accept wages and conditions that are below the minimum standards, and will have no recourse to the law. Many illegal migrants, especially women, are forced into work that is dangerous, dirty and demeaning, including sex work.

The communications revolution and the physical migration of people has led to talk about *a new global culture*, carried by television, pop music, films, books and the internet, as well as consumer goods like Gap clothes, Coke and McDonald's fast foods. Culture in these forms is bought and sold and the market is dominated by the consumer values of wealthy countries. However, some cultural traditions from the developing world have also spread into the West as countries become more multi-ethnic, for instance cuisine (Indian, Chinese, Thai) or music (Caribbean, African). Developing understanding of this aspect of globalisation should not present difficulties to teachers with a feel for a multicultural curriculum.

Multinationals are also responsible for global integration. Increasingly, large companies do not export their goods but establish factories abroad staffed by local people, in both the developing and the developed world. When multinationals establish industries in the developing world, they may take advantage of low wages and the absence of unions to exploit people and keep their profits high. They are also accused of trampling on local customs and creating demand for the consumer products of the West which replace established traditions. But the multinationals also bring technological know-how and new social values – particularly about women. This does not mean that multinationals should not be criticised. Using one's power as a consumer and invoking human rights conventions may be the most fruitful way to protect people in developing countries from damage and exploitation by multinationals. As with the issue of migrant workers, children can be made aware and add their voice to protest against human rights violations, particularly when they themselves are the beneficiaries of exploitation.

Domination by the West is evident in *global management and governance*. The developing countries do not have an equal voice in the big institutions which make international policy such as the World Bank, the International Monetary Fund, G8 and the World Trade Organisation. These institutions tend to be strong on protecting technology and markets, but have made much less progress in human rights. It is not possible to predict where issues will arise in the future; contemporary cases will always be preferable to raise with children than those dating from before they can remember. However, possible case studies from the past decade or so include the case of Shell's human rights and environmental record in Nigeria and the murder of Ken Saro-Wiwa, or the Bhopal disaster in 1984, which implicated the huge multinational Union Carbide: the terrible effects of the gas leaks on people's health are still evident.

According to the UN Report on Human Development, the NGOs should take significant credit for giving people a voice in human rights matters in both the North and the South. They have maintained pressure on national and international agencies to keep human rights commitments and environmental standards and have managed to reverse policy on some of the issues adverse to the poor, for example the successful campaign to reduce the price of Aids/HIV drugs for South Africa. Since empowering children, rather than making them feel utterly helpless, should be part of one's aim in global citizenship education, they could learn about the work of the NGOs and understand how they can participate actively in their programmes.

Sustainable development and global threats to the environment

The environmental emergency has global dimensions which cannot be tackled by any single national government. Moreover, the poorer nations are more threatened by environmental degradation than the rich, partly because some environmental threats are taking place within their borders (eg deforestation), partly because they are less equipped to cope when disaster strikes – a typhoon, earthquake or flood. It is important for children to realise that environmental degradation will affect us all, making no allowances for national borders, and that it is imperative to see ourselves as part of the global economy. Children should be encouraged to understand where, as responsible consumers, they fit into the environmental picture, and to add their voice to the demand for less destructive processes.

Global threats to security and health

The shrinking world has been exploited by 'bad guys' who have created illegal global markets in drugs, crime and weapons. International crime syndicates are sometimes at the bottom of illegal trafficking in women and girls for sex work and financing pornography. The illegal market in weapons is still destabilising societies, from Albania to southern Africa. Increasingly, in what feels like a return to the Middle Ages, local wars are fought not by national armies but by hired mercenaries. The international drugs trade impacts on all societies, whether consumers or producers. Consumption of hard drugs incurs enormous costs on health and welfare and is associated with crime. The drugs barons are in a position to exploit growers of the raw materials, such as opium poppies and coca leaves, since the growers often have no other form of livelihood (eg in Colombia, Afghanistan). These examples illustrate the relationship between repressive governments, the absence of human rights and poverty.

HIV/Aids is the plague of the late twentieth and early twenty first centuries and affects the poorest nations disproportionately. HIV/Aids is linked to trans-national travel, including migrant work, as well as to attitudes about protected sex, exploitation of young girls and lack of medicines at affordable prices, which are characteristic of developing countries.

Teaching children about global inequality and the effects of globalisation

Oxfam's curriculum for global citizenship starts with the following statement:

> The young people of today will grow up to be the citizens of the future: but what that future holds for them is not yet clear. The world they live in is one of tremendous change and opportunity but also one of increasing inequality. While many people enjoy a higher standard of living than ever before, many others – both in the UK and overseas – face life without enough to eat, without a home, without freedom from violence, without a way of earning a living, without a say in their future. Oxfam believes that poverty is at the root of all these problems ... extreme poverty ... is also inefficient. It wastes human talent, leads to conflict and unrest and encourages the destruction of scarce environmental resources.

The document then focuses on values and attitudes which will contribute to children developing as 'global citizens' so that they can challenge poverty and injustices and, it is alleged, take real effective action. Children need some principles which will help them think through how change might be effected and make them more than banner wavers.

Many children are deeply concerned about the environment; familiar themes in primary schools, such as deforestation or dumping of waste materials, can be the vehicle to help children understand the link between human poverty and human rights. A large multinational company or a local government which is laying forests bare or dumping pollutants in the local waters is doing more than destroy the environment. These actions will involve large-scale enterprises which affect existing local livelihoods and opportunities – the work people do, the housing or lack of it provided, the pay they receive, the conditions they work in, which can be inhumane and hazardous. One can ask if such enterprises are also supporting repressive regimes financially and morally, and thus, at one remove, undermining human rights.

Global citizenship requires children to do far more than espouse charitable attitudes and be willing to donate pocket-money or raise funds for specific causes or individuals. A model based on individualised charity as the solution to entrenched global imbalance is sadly outdated, even if it is still necessary and appropriate for certain acute disasters. Using teaching material from the main NGOs, children can debate channelling international aid towards primary education, self-help and anti-poverty projects. Case studies focus on what inequality means for ordinary people, how poverty is 'gendered'. Using these materials, children can address some of the themes in this chapter, with honesty about the down-side and the up-side of change. They can develop awareness and understanding about the causes of poverty and discrimination within our own relatively rich society and the connections with globalisation. And so we come full circle, to address the starting point of this book – abuse of each other's families rooted in racism and ignorance about economic inequality. The hope is that we can replace pious admonitions to be nicer to one another with genuine understanding about human rights and care and compassion for the less fortunate.

8

Resources for use in schools and classrooms

This selection of resources provides a starting point and does not claim to be comprehensive. Material of variable quality on citizenship education is pouring onto the market. I have included material which I personally liked, including some fiction and poetry for children. All the academic/adult material referenced in this book can be found in the bibliography.

It is also worth checking the current Letterbox Library Catalogue (books by mail order).

Letterbox Library – celebrating equality and diversity in the best children's books,
71-73 Allen Road
London N.16 8RY
Telephone 0207.503.4801
Email info@letterboxlibrary.com
www.letterboxlibrary.com

Sections in this Resources List

1. Circle time – self-esteem and collaboration in the classroom
2. Citizenship issues – mostly personal and local
3. Emotional literacy and sensitive personal issues
4. Environmental and global issues
5. Human Rights and Children's Rights

6. Refugees
7. Religion
8. Tackling homophobia and heterosexism
9. Thinking skills, Philosophy for Children

CIRCLE TIME – SELF-ESTEEM AND COLLABORATION IN THE CLASSROOM

Bliss, T, Maines, B and Robinson, G, 1995, *Developing Circle Time*, Lucky Duck Publishing

Clearly written activities. Different emphases to Mosley (below) – more concerned with confidentiality and feelings; less about behaviour management.

Borsa, Michele, 1989, *Esteem Builders: a K-8 self esteem curriculum for improving student achievement, behaviour and school climate*, Jalmar Press, California

American; practical and easy-to-use activities for KS2/3 classrooms

Burns, S and Lamont, G, 2000, *Values and Visions: Who are you? Who am I? An antiracist programme for schools*, Hodder and Stoughton with DEP, Cafod and Christian Aid

Takes on bad feeling between different groups; self-esteem and identity of refugees; why people live in Britain; culture and customs.

Button, K and Winter, M, no date, *Pushing back the furniture: practical ways of teaching social skills, developing co-operation and enhancing self esteem in the primary classroom*, Behaviour Support Service, Kirklees Education Authority

Gust, John, 1994, *Enhancing self-esteem: a whole language approach*, Good Apple, Paramount Publishing

Activities clearly set out.

Hobbs, Nancy, 2000, *Project Charlie: PSHE*, Drugs Education

Based on the drugs education programme Hobbs carries out in primary schools; excellent practical activities for work on self-esteem, relationships, decision-making and resisting peer pressure. Order direct from Nancy Hobbs, 102 Buckingham Road, London N.1, 4JE

Mosley, J, 1996, *Quality Circle Time*, LDA
1998, *More Quality Circle Time*, LDA
1998, *Turn your school around*, LDA

Practical, clear, easy to implement, from the most well-known theorist and trainer for circle time in the UK. Mosley's approach emphasises reward systems and removal of privileges for transgressing rules.

CITIZENSHIP ISSUES, MOSTLY PERSONAL AND LOCAL

www.citfou.org.uk Citizenship Foundation

www.citizenorg.uk Institute for Citizenship

www.cewc/org.uk Council for Education of World Citizenship

www.csv.org.uk Community Service Volunteers

www.schoolscouncils.org Schools Councils UK

www.le.ac.uk/education/centres Centre for Citizenship Studies in Education at Leicester University

www.cypf.org Children and Youth Partnership Foundation

Allen, JoBeth (ed) 1999, *Teaching for Social Justice in Elementary and Middle Schools*, Teachers College Press

American; excellent ideas and classroom activities.

Barnickle, Carole and Wilson, Duncan, 2000, *Me as a Citizen*, Hopscotch Ed Publishers

Photo-copiable activities for KS2

Barry, A and Griffith, A, 1998, *Citizens of the Future: activities for English, Careers and PSE*, Folens Publications

Excellent for KS3 and 4; some adaptable for KS2

Brookes, K., 1999, *Young Citizen at Home*, Wayland

Cartoon format, quizzes, activities and questions – very accessible for KS2 and early KS3

Brookes, K, 1999, *Young Citizen at School*, Wayland

Rules, respect for self and others, gangs and peer pressure, improving the school

Brookes, K, 2000, *Young Citizen Growing Up*, Wayland

Mostly about relationships and changes at puberty

Brookes, K, 2000, *Young Citizen in the Street*, Wayland

Good neighbourliness, getting on with parents, peer pressure

Clough, Nick and Holden, Cathie, 2001, *Education for Citizenship: ideas into action – a practical guide for teachers of pupils aged 7-14*, Routledge/Falmer

Summarises research as well as offering practical guidance and photocopiable material. Covers the full range of possible work on citizenship, including working through the English, Geography and History curricula, and a section on global dimensions.

Institute for Citizenship, 2000, *Citizenship for Primary Schools, Teachers' Resource Books for Years 3-4 and Years 5-6*, Nelson Thornes

Rowe, D *et al*, 1998, *Citizenship for all*, Citizenship Foundation

More for KS3 than KS2; useful scenarios and discussion points

Rowe, D and Newton, J, 1994, *You, me, us: social and moral responsibility for primary schools*, Citizenship Foundation.

Highly recommended for working with KS2

EMOTIONAL LITERACY AND SENSITIVE PERSONAL ISSUES

www.antidote.org.uk – manifesto and resources

www.dialogueworks.co.uk – a UK based site on philosophy with children which is also concerned with emotional literacy. (See the Marshmallow listening project)

The Place to Be, Edinburgh House, 154-182 Kennington Lane, London SE.11, 4EZ, 020.7820.6487 is an organization which provides information for setting up one-to-one support in a secure small group for children with emotional difficulties.

Danziger, Paula and Martin, Ann, 1999, *Snailmail no more: a novel by email*, Hodder Children's Books,

The sequel to *Longer letter later*, 1999. Elizabeth writes to Tara about the emotional turmoil caused by her alcoholic father.

Elliot, Pat, 1997, *Coping with Loss: for parents*, Piccadilly Press

Though written for parents, this is suitable for anyone. Deals with a variety of changes, transitions and losses in a child's life, including preparation for death, bereavement itself and grief.

Fine, A, 1992, *Flour Babies*, Penguin

Carnegie Award winner. The book is about young secondary school boys, but it's accessible to younger children. The 'thick class' has to look after 6 lb. 'flour babies' for three weeks as part of a science project. Simon Martin, champion footballer, whose father walked out when he was 6 weeks old, develops an extraordinary emotional attachment for his flour baby, discovers that you mustn't have babies till you're really ready, considers his own potential to be a good father, and starts to understand why his father left.

Fine, A, 1995, *Step by Wicked Step*, Puffin.

On a school journey five pupils from reconstituted families tell their tales. Includes perspectives of adults on how hard it can be to be a stepmother or father, not just a stepchild.

Fine, A, 1996, *The Tulip Touch*, Puffin (Whitbread Children's Book of the Year)

Explanations for Tulip's weird antisocial behaviour are subtly attributed to the cruel and abusive behaviour she suffers at home from a tyrannical father.

Holbrook, Sara, 1998, *Walking on the Boundaries of Change: Poems of Transition*, Boyds Mills Press (Coretta Scott King Honours Book)

Poems that confront and question difficult choices, transition, pressure and lies.

McGough, Roger (ed) 1999, *Poems about Love*, Kingfisher

Not just about love, the poems provide starting points for work on self-esteem, friendship, loneliness, hope, death, dreams. KS2

Wilson, Jacqueline, 2000, *The Illustrated Mum*, Corgi Yearling

Funny and poignant – living with a manic-depressive mother. Guardian Children's Fiction Award winner.

Woodson, Jacqueline, 1994, *I hadn't meant to tell you this*, Bantam Doubleday

Two girls, one black, one white, both with no mother, become friends. One has a dreadful secret. A book about racism, child abuse and survival, and the dilemma of keeping your word to your friend about confidentiality, even when she is in danger.

ENVIRONMENTAL AND GLOBAL ISSUES

www.foe.co.uk Friends of the Earth

www.oxfam.org.uk Oxfam

www.globaldimension.org.uk Department for International Development (DFID)

www.tidec.org Teachers in development education (Birmingham based). Good for resources for KS2 and 3 and 'think pieces'

www.dep.org.uk Development Education Project

www.devedassoc@gn.apc.org Development Education Association

Burns, S and Lamont, G, 2000, *Values and Visions: spiritual development and global awareness*, Hodder and Stoughton with DEF, CAFOD and Christian Aid.

Strong antiracist approach; trialled in primary schools in Manchester.

DEA, 1995, *Global Perspectives in the National Curriculum: Guidance for Key Stages 1 and 2*

Summary of opportunities for teaching and learning about global issues across the curriculum within the primary National Curriculum.

DEA, 2001, *Black Voices in Development Education*

Description of a variety of black-led projects in Britain relating to development.

Department for International Development/DfEE/QCA/The Central Bureau, 2000, *Developing a global dimension in the school curriculum*

Useful page of key concepts summarised under each curriculum area.

Marsden, J and Tan, S, 1998, *The Rabbits*, Thomas Lothian Ltd (Picture Book of the Year, Australia)

An extraordinary allegory which relies on the illustrations rather than text, questioning colonisation, 'progress' and the destruction of existing societies

Morgan, Sally, 1998, *Genetic Engineering – moral dilemmas series*, Evans

Discusses GM foods, cloning, research ethics; KS2/3

OXFAM Development Education Programme, no date, *A Curriculum for Global Citizenship*, Oxfam

Knowledge and understanding, skills, values and attitudes from Foundation Stage through to 16-19, set out in a clear chart.

PACHAMAMA – our earth – our future, 1999, U.N. Environment Project and Evans

Pachamama means mother earth in Inca. An illustrated book of children's reports; includes the human interventions at the root of some environmental issues.

HUMAN RIGHTS AND CHILDREN'S RIGHTS

It is not possible to list all the non-governmental voluntary organisations and charity sites concerned with human rights and children's rights. Add the names of charities that you support or have found useful.

www.amnesty.org.uk

www.blink.org.uk – umbrella for a number of black-led voluntary organisations

www.carelinkinternational.org.uk – relief and care organization particularly active with survivors of natural disasters and war – eg projects in Gujarat after the earthquake in 2000, regeneration and redevelopment in Bosnia

www.comicrelief.com/education has a variety of lesson plans and a children's interactive site

www.crin.org – Children's Rights Information Network. Takes you into resources and information sections

www.dep.org.uk – Development Education Project

www.demos.co.uk – independent research and think tank on community action, foreign policy and radical solutions to problems in society; includes projects for school, research on children in Britain

www.derechos.net – useful international site on human rights, presented in an accessible format

www.redcross.org.uk – projects in Britain as well as abroad

www.savethechildren.org.uk – useful for their newest resources including material for use in schools

www.shelter.org.uk – one of the main charities in Britain concerned with homelessness

www.torturecare.org.uk – the Medical Foundation for the Victims of Torture cares for adults and children who have been physically and psychologically damaged by regimes that do not respect human rights, and has case studies and information which would develop understanding without causing nightmares

www.undp.org – United National Development Programme; contains full reports indispensable for up to date information and policy round the world

www.uhchr.org – UN High Commission for Human Rights

www.ycare.org.uk – branch of the YMCA working on long-term intervention projects with the poorest young people, for world development

Bradley, Catherine, 1997, *What do we mean by human rights: freedom of movement,* Franklin Watts

Nationality, refugees' rights to work abroad: case studies – photos and personal stories. KS3 and 4 and older KS2

Brown, Margot (ed) 1996, *Our World, our right: teaching about rights and responsibilities in the primary school*, Amnesty International.

One of the first and still one of the best handbooks of information, activities, case studies and starting points for discussion. Includes the texts of the Children's Rights Convention, the Universal Declaration on Human Rights and good resource lists.

Brown, Margot and Harrison, Don, 1996, *Changing Childhoods – a sourcebook for teaching 8-12s about children and social change in Britain since the 1930s*, Save the Children with the Centre for Global Education

Development Education Project and UNICEF 1999, *Talking Rights: Taking Responsibility: a speaking and listening resource for secondary English and citizenship*

Scenarios, games, discussion. Takes on controversial and conflictual issues, stereotyping, identity. Can easily be used for KS2

Development Education Project, 2000, *Take Part! Speak Out! Education for citizenship in primary schools*

Sections on rights and responsibilities, justice and power, how democracy works, discussion and argument skills, detection of bias

Dunbar, Katrina, 2000, *What's at Issue: citizenship and you*, Heinemann

Human rights, equality, democracy, making laws.

Fountain, Susan, 1993, *It's only right – a practical guide to learning about the convention on the rights of the child,* UNICEF

Fox, C, Leysen, A and Koenders, A, (eds) 2000, *In Times of War*, Pavilion

An anthology of war literature from a variety of authors including Raymond Briggs, Art Spiegelman and Michael Morpugo

Gray, A, 2000, *What's at Issue – Right or Wrong?* Heinemann

Personal issues and bigger issues like euthanasia, drugs, aid, protest, terrorism

Harrison, M and Stuart-Clarke, C (eds) 1989, *Peace and War: a collection of poems*, Oxford University Press

Some well-known poets, others less familiar. Accessibility and difficulty varies. Some good starting points for KS2 as well as KS3

Haughton, E and Clarke, P, 1997, *What do we mean by human rights: rights in the home,* Franklin Watts

Equal rights in marriage, gay relationships, caring for the elderly, children's rights, domestic violence; KS3 and 4; adapt or use selectively in KS2. Not activity-based but well written and illustrated; teachers would need to develop activities

Jewish Council for Racial Equality, 1999, *Let's Make a Difference: teaching antiracism in primary schools – a Jewish perspective,* JCORE

For KS1 and 2 – practical and interesting activities around identity, roots, moving, being new/different, multicultural Britain, stereotyping and racism, and making a difference.

Klein, Reva, 2001, *Citizens by Right,* Save the Children and Trentham

Teaching citizenship in primary school from a human rights perspective.

Kramer, A, 1988, *Women in Politics,* Wayland

An opportunity to raise issues of human rights and struggles for women's equality through selected historical issues from the C19th and C20th.

Rees, B and Sherwood, M, 1998, *Black Peoples of the Americas,* Heinemann

The history of black struggle for human rights is a very big issue. I have chosen one book for this resources list which meets criteria for careful perspectives, quotations, reproductions of original sources. KS2 and 3

Save the Children, 2001, *Partners in Rights: creative activities exploring rights and citizenship for 7-11 year olds*

Uses creative and expressive art work on Latin America, the Caribbean and the UK to develop ideas of children's rights and global citizenship. KS2

Stand up for your rights, 1998, Peace Child International

Each article of the Human Rights Convention illustrated in words and pictures by children from around the world. Issues and controversies for debate

Stearman, Kaye, 1993. *Human Rights: Freedom of Expression*, Wayland

International perspectives on this basic human right. Photographic evidence and issues for discussion and comparison, for example Burma's suppression of Aung San Suu Kyi, neo-Nazi marches in Berlin, protests in America against Gulf War

Steele, Philip, 1997, *What do we mean by human rights: Freedom of Speech*, Franklin Watts

Soweto and the rebellion against learning Afrikaans; censorship, how to respond to overt racism, adverts, exploitation of women, protest and demonstration; KS3 and 4 and older KS2. Not activity-based but well written and illustrated; teachers would need to develop activities

Zephaniah, Benjamin, 2000, *Wicked World*, Puffin.

Zephaniah's incomparable poetry provides starting points for discussion about conditions in other countries, national identity, human rights, refugees

Please see the extensive resources section in my previous book, *Reclaiming our Pasts*, Trentham, 1996, for resources for children on black activists and women in the human rights struggle, and also for fiction on these issues.

Adult resources

Klein, Naomi, 2001, *No Logo*, Flamingo

Best-seller giving information about the multinationals, the big brand names and campaigns to limit their power. Also useful for work on global issues

Save the Children, 2000, *Children's Rights, Equal Rights? Diversity, difference and the issue of discrimination*, Save the Children

Information about children the world over, recommendations about change for individual countries to comply with Convention on Rights of the Child. Contains the Convention on Rights of the Child in full

REFUGEES

www.refugeecouncil.org.uk – case histories and resources created specially for schools

Ashley, B, 1999, *Little Soldier*, Orchard Books

Hard-hitting story of a child soldier rescued by a Christian charity and brought to England; KS2/3

Anderson, Rachel, 1987, *The War Orphan*, Swallow, Richard Drew Publishing

Gripping story based on fact, of a young casualty of the Vietnam war. Language probably too difficult for most KS2 readers, unless very fluent

Burns Knight, Margy, 1993, *Who belongs here?* Tilbury House Publications

American, based on story of a Cambodian refugee. Good starting point for discussion about treatment of refugees and immigration, and reasons for leaving one's original country. KS2

Gibbons, A, 1999, *A fight to belong: a true story*, Save the Children

The campaign to prevent deportation of a Nigerian family and the support given by the school. Accessible, first person narrative. KS2

Hasbubak, Zeynap and Simons, Brian, 1986, *Zeynap: that really happened to me*, ALTARF

How William Patten Primary School in Hackney took on the threatened deportation of one of their Turkish pupils and her family. A classic.

Hicyilmaz, Gaye, 1998, *Smiling for Strangers*, Dolphin paperback, Orion Children's Books

A refugee from Sarajevo makes her way to political asylum in England. Gripping, graphic and well written; for top KS2/3

Kerr, Judith, 1989, *When Hitler Stole Pink Rabbit*, Collins

Another classic, fiction based on Kerr's own story of escaping from Nazi Germany. KS2

Naidoo, B, 2000, *The other side of truth*, Puffin

Carnegie Award Winner. Sade and Femi, refugees from Nigeria, face bullying and ignorance in their new English schools. Provides insights into the plight of asylum seekers in Britain. Top KS2

Rutter, Jill, 1991, *Refugees: we left because we had to – an educational book for 14 – 18 year olds*, Refugee Council

Activities, scenarios and role plays. Includes cartoon format histories of Vietnamese, Kurdish, Afghani, Palestinian and Tamil refugees. Raises human rights questions and challenges prejudices. Easily adaptable or appropriate for KS2

Rutter, Jill, 1992, *Refugees: a resource book for 8-13 year olds*, Refugee Council

Activities, cartoon stories, photos, real stories.

Wilkes, Sybella, 1994, *One day we had to run*, UNHCR and Save the Children

Children's own stories, drawings, information pages: based on Sudanese, Somalian and Ethiopian refugees

Adult Resources

Richman, Naomi, 1998, *In the midst of the whirlwind; a manual for helping refugee children*, Trentham Books

An educational pychologist identifies the needs of the children and how they can be met.

Rutter, Jill, 2001, *Supporting refugee children in the classroom: a compendium for teachers*, Trentham

Essential information about the 35 most recent refugee groups in our schools and examples of good practice in schools and local authorities

RELIGION

Ganeri, Anita, 1998, *What's the big idea? Religion*, Hodder Children's Books

Concentrates on moral issues and ethics rather than festivals or practices. Cartoons give an accessible, light touch. Includes debating points such as 'Is there a God? If so, why is there so much evil and suffering in the world?'

Ganeri, Anita, 1998, *Journey's End: death and mourning,* Evans

Customs and practices and beliefs including the afterlife, from the six main religions

Strickland, T, 2000, *A child's Book of Prayers*, Barefoot Books Ltd

Prayers from around the world from the major and less well known religions, with beautiful photographs of children.

TACKLING HOMOPHOBIA AND HETEROSEXISM

Greenberg, Keith, 1996, *Zack's Story, growing up with same sex parents,* Lerner Publications Company, Minneapolis.

First person narrative with appealing photographs, about an 11 year old living with lesbian parents

Heron, Ann and Maran, Meredith, 1991, *How would you feel if your Dad was gay?* Alyson Publications, New York (available in Britain through Turnaround Publication Services)

Eleven year old African-American children face and take on homophobic prejudices of their classmates. Drawings and accessible text

Newman, L, 1993, *Saturday is Pattyday*, Women's Press

A young boy copes with the separation of his lesbian parents.

Newman, L, 2000, *Heather has two mommies*, Alyson Publications, N.Y.

For young KS2 and KS1

Valentine, Johnny, 1993, *Two Moms, the Zark and me*, Alyson Publications, N.Y.

Appropriate for quite young children, amusing rhyming text with cartoon-type pictures

Vigna, J, 1995, *My two uncles*, Albert Whitman and Co. N.Y.

A simple picture book which takes on family prejudice against gays (young KS2/1)

Woodson, Jacqueline, 1995, *From the notebooks of Melanin Sun, Scholastic* (Coretta Scott King Honours Book, Jane Addams Peace Award, 1996)

> One of the few good novels for older primary age children which deals with homophobia. Written partly as a diary, it's about a young black boy on the cusp of adolescence, living in Brooklyn with his lesbian mother

THINKING SKILLS, PHILOSOPHY FOR CHILDREN

www.sapere.net Philosophy with Children.

www.utasedu.audocs.humsoc/philosophy Useful and interesting Australian site.

www.somersetthinkingskills.co.uk Small, but informative set of papers about theory and on-going work.

www.teachingthinking.net Dr Bob Fisher's Centre for Thinking Skills (CRITT) at Brunel University which runs PIPS – Philosophy in Primary Schools

philip.adey@kcl.ac.uk Professor Adey, Centre for the Advancement of Thinking, at Kings College, London University, has revived and extended much of the material which primary teachers used in the 1970s and 80s (before the Literacy and Numeracy Strategies) through a research programme on cognitive acceleration to develop logical thought.

Fisher, Robert, 1996, *Stories for Thinking*, Nash Pollock
1997, *Games for Thinking*, Nash Pollock

Fox, Richard, 1996, *Thinking Matters – stories to encourage thinking skills*, Southgate

Murris, Karen, 1995, *Teaching philosophy with picture books*, Infonet

Adult resources

Fisher, Robert, 1995, *Teaching Children to Learn*, Stanley Thornes

Lipman, Mathew, 1988, *Philosophy goes to school*, Temple University Press

Matthews G, 1984, *Dialogues with Children,* Harvard,
1994, *The Philosophy of Childhood*, 1994, Harvard

Both these are readable introductions to Philosophy with Children

Quinn, Victor, 1997, *Critical Thinking in Young Minds*, David Fulton

APPENDIX
The interview schedule

Introduction

- My name, a bit about myself and what I'm doing (writing a book about children's ideas, have written some other books).
- Anything you'd like to ask before we begin? (Children tended to ask about other books I'd written, when this one would get published, whether I had children of my own.)
- I put the questions on the table in front of us and asked the children if they'd like to read them (or have me read them) before we started. Some said yes, some said no. Children could choose which questions we started with, or leave some out.
- Is it OK to go on with this now or do you want to stop and go back to your classroom?
- I'd like you just to chat together about the following things. Take as long as you like about each thing and don't feel you have to rush on to the next one. Try and say as much as you are able to, to explain how you feel.
- There aren't any right or wrong answers – just say what you think and feel.

The questions

Would you like to change anything in school life for children?

Would you like to change anything around where you live if you could?

Would you like to change anything in your family? (Repeated that they needn't answer this if they didn't want to.)

Why do people get into fights and arguments?

Why do peoples and countries go to war?

What are your views about this?

What makes you happy about how other people behave?

What makes you sad about how other people behave?

What makes you angry about how other people behave?

Do you think adults and children are very different? Please say as much as you can.

What sorts of things are you concerned about (do you care about)?

What do you think is the most important thing in life? (Explained that this question had come from a child.)

Would most people agree with you?

If you'd been making up these questions, what would you have asked the children? (I then wrote down their questions, and asked each pair the questions they had posed.)

Before you finish, is there anything you feel strongly about that you haven't had a chance to say?

Thank you very much for your help.

References

Billig, M. (1987) *Arguing and thinking: a rhetorical approach to social psychology*, Cambridge University Press, Cambridge.

Billig, M. and others (1988) *Ideological Dilemmas: A social psychology of everyday thinking*, Sage, London.

Blair, M. and Bourne, J. (1998) *Making the difference: teaching and learning strategies in successful multi-ethnic schools*, Open University with DfEE.

Bonnett, M. (1994) *Children's thinking: promoting understanding in the primary school*, Cassell, London.

Bruner, J. (1979) *On Knowing: Essays for the left hand*, Harvard Univ Press, Cambridge Mass.

Bruner, J. (1991) The narrative construction of reality, *Critical Inquiry*, 18, 1-21.

Claire, H. (1996) *Reclaiming our Pasts: equality and diversity in the primary history curriculum*, Trentham, Stoke on Trent.

Crick, B. (1998) *Education for citizenship and the teaching of democracy in schools: Final Report of the Advisory Group on Citizenship*, QCA, London.

Dean, J. S. C. (2001) Coping with Curriculum Change in South Africa, *International Journal of History Teaching and Learning and Research*, 1.

DfEE/QCA (1999a) *Citizenship Key Stages 3 – 4, The National Curriculum for England*, QCA/DfEE, London.

DfEE/QCA (1999b) *The National Curriculum for England Key Stages 1 and 2*, DfEE/QCA, London.

DfEE/QCA (2000) *History Teacher's guide. Update. A scheme of work for Key Stages 1 and 2*, QCA, London.

Freeman, M. (1993) *Rewriting the Self: history, memory, narrative*, Routledge, London.

Gilligan, C. (1982) *In a Different Voice: psychological theory and women's development*, Harvard University Press, Cambridge, Mass.

Gilligan, C., Ward, J., Taylor, J. and Bardige, B. (Eds.) (1988) *Mapping the Moral Domain*, Harvard University Press, Cambridge, Mass.

Goleman, D. (1996) *Emotional Intelligence: why it can matter more than IQ*, Bloomsbury, London.

Hines, V. (1998) *How Black People overcame 50 years of Repression in Britain Vol 1:1945-1975*, Zulu Publications, London.

Holden, C. (1999) *Education for Citizenship: the contribution of social, moral and cultural education in children's and young people's social, political and economic learning and understanding within the European context* (Ed. CiCe) University of North London School of Education/CiCe, London.

Kelly, E. and Cohn, T. (1989) *Racism in Schools: new research evidence*, Trentham, Stoke on Trent.

Klein, N. (2001) *No Logo*, Flamingo, HarperCollins, London.

Macpherson, W. (1999) *The Stephen Lawrence Inquiry: report of an inquiry by Sir William Macpherson of Cluny*, HMSO, London.

Maslow, A. (1968) *Towards a Psychology of Being*, Van Nostrand, New York.

McGoughlin, T. (1992) Citizenship, diversity and education: a philosophical perspective, *Journal of Moral Education*, 21, 235-250.

Midgley, M. (1991) *Can't we make Moral Judgements?* The Bristol Press, Bristol.

Midgley, M. (1997) Can education be moral? in *Teaching Right and Wrong* (Eds. Smith, R. and Standish, P.) Trentham, Stoke on Trent.

Naidoo, B. (1985) *Journey to Jo'burg*, HarperCollins, London.

Neuberger, J. (1995) *On being Jewish*, Heinemann, London.

Noddings, N. (1984) *Caring: a feminine approach to ethics and moral education*, University of California Press, Berkeley.

Osler, A. (Ed.) (2000) *Citizenship and Democracy in Schools: diversity, identity, equality,* Trentham, Stoke on Trent.

Parekh, B. (2000) *The Future of Multi-Ethnic Britain: Report of the Commission on the Future of Multi-Ethnic Britain*, Runnymede Trust/Profile Books, London.

QCA (2000a) *Personal, Social and Health Education and Citizenship at Key Stages 1 and 2: Initial guidance for schools*, QCA, London.

QCA (2000b) *Religious Education: Non-statutory guidance on RE 5 – 16*, QCA, London.

Rawls, J. (1999) *John Rawls: Collected Papers*, edited by S. Freeman, Harvard University Press, London

Smail, D. (1993) *The Origins of Unhappiness: a new understanding of personal distress*, HarperCollins, London.

Taylor, M. (1998) *Values Education and Values in Education: a guide to the issues commissioned by ATL*, Association of Teachers and Lecturers and NFER.

Torres, C. A. (1998) *Democracy, Education and Multiculturalism: dilemmas of citizenship in a global world*, Rowman and Littlefield Publishers Inc, Oxford.

United Nations Development Programme (2000) *Human Development Report*, United Nations.

Index